KINGDOM COME

A Book of Threes

David Udom

CHAINBREAKER
PUBLISHING

In memory of Mr. Thomas Simpson

1931 – 2007

CONTENTS

AUTHOR'S NOTE

T here is nothing new under the sun.
At first glance, these words appear to belong to a simpler time. Our era of burgeoning technological break-throughs and easier access to remote places, both physical and intellectual, would aspire to snap this generation's picture through a more sophisticated lens.

However, a closer look reveals the complex truth within those simple words. Life has a pattern, a method embedded in loops of events that keep recurring, like a giant Slinky flipping down the stairs, creating identical arches as it lopes its way into the future.

We are, quite simply, new actors recycling old ideas, in different combinations, at different points in time.

And through it all, people still succumb to disease and play with toys; air is still breathed; seasons still change; blood still runs red; and no matter how bad things get, there is still love in the world.

Being a Christian by birth and, more recently, by choice, I see King Solomon's view on the repetitious nature of life through a creationist filter. In other words, if all creation took place in six days, both physical and spiritual, then all ideas have already been created. Looked at that way, old King Sully makes perfect sense, really.

By the same token, if God created man and woman in his own image, man's best efforts at life and relationships can only be realized by learning more about who God really is. It also is plausible that being human means unconsciously creating snapshots of heaven, by establishing copies of God's relationships.

This book explores these relationships, through a recurrent pattern of allegories and scriptural interpretations.

My observations are an exercise in personal preference, and the Bible quotes used throughout the book will make it feel more familiar to a certain type of audience. But you do not have to start out a Christian in the traditional sense to be an earnest, uncompromising seeker of the truth. If you are such a one, this book is for you.

Indeed, many traditionally classified Christians disagree with me on this point, but it is my contention that if you are a sincere apprentice of the truth, you are a Christian.

Happy reading.

PROLOGUE

G od never made a bad day in his life.

That is a complete truth. It also is the hardest thing to remember sometimes. After an exhausting day of running behind on what should have been routine tasks; seemingly endless demands on a very finite supply of patience; and hours speckled with a few computer crashes that make you wonder why the stupid instrument was invented in the first place; it's officially a bad day.

A knock on the door, and a somewhat flustered man looked up to see and greet yet another client. Banal verbal pleasantries were exchanged, automatic smiles worn. He sized up the day's new challenge.

His automatic inspection revealed a portly, elderly Caucasian male in his seventies. Neither tall, nor short; a nondescript dresser. The kind of guy you see every day, absentmindedly smile at, and promptly relegate to the foggy attic of life's experiences, the ones you never consciously revisit. He was that kind of man, until you noticed the bright twinkle in his eye.

The new guy was a talker.

"I heard you were a good man, so I came to see you."

Not today, I'm not.

"Do you know I am a Bible scholar?" The old man chortled, prattling away as his younger audience listened politely, intermittently tuning out with no change in facial expression. Or, at least, so he hoped.

"...worked with some Germans on the building site. Used to tease them about Adolph Hitler all the time. Do you know why Hitler lost the war?"

Silence.

Oops! I'm supposed to contribute here. How on earth did we get on the topic of Hitler?

"No. Why?"

"Because he was messing with spiritual matters when he decided to create a one-thousand year Reich. He was trying to do what Jesus will do after he returns. Big mistake."

"Hmm. I never thought of it that way. Interesting." He leaned back, looking over at the cheerful old man, enjoying the rambling conversation despite himself.

"I watched an interview. You know, old clips of Hitler's interviews from the thirties. The interviewer asked him how he got so many people to follow him. Do you know what he said?"

"No."

"All I need is one third. Then I'll get the second third. Then, I've won."

The old man seemed to be done, and rose up from his chair. Verbal pleasantries were exchanged once again, engaging smiles worn. The strange old man, a satisfied, *completed* look on his lined face, walked away, with that ponderous gait characteristic of toddlers and the elderly. He was watched thoughtfully by his audience of one, the man who could have had a bad day, but didn't.

That was the day he knew he had to write a book on threes and thirds.

A BOOK OF THREES, THIRDS, AND MODERN ALLEGORIES

SECTION I

THE YOUNG MOTORIST

A drenaline is a powerful substance.

It would make giants out of mere men. Without adrenaline, things would probably have gone quite differently. But the heady elixir exists, and was currently coursing—in large quantities—through the veins of a certain young head.

The vehicle had already stalled once, a state of affairs which might have given a lesser mortal pause. Not this one. The youth forged ahead, hastily wiping sweaty palms on ancient denim pants.

"Key in the ignition."

Check.

"Seat belt on."

Check.

"Turn signal lights working."

Check.

"Gas gauge on full."

Check.

"Windshield wipers working properly?"

Check.

"All right." A deep cleansing breath as nervous, youthful fingers gripped the steering wheel's unyielding rim. "All right, let's do this."

A quick, slightly jerky twist of the key in the ignition, first hesitantly counterclockwise, then clockwise, several times.

But the stubborn key would not budge. "Okay, what now?" A raggedy run-down of the list of "to-dos" and "to-don'ts." "Ah, pea brain! Put it back in park."

This time, a powerful, throaty growl erupted from the sleek automobile in response to a twist of the ignition key, quickly fading to a muted purring, as the powerful engine turned over smoothly and effortlessly. "Okay baby, let's roll!"

Heralded by a momentary screeching whine, the car leapt backwards with herky-jerky speed as the driver put the gear shift in reverse and pumped the gas pedal with a somewhat hasty right foot.

"Oh, no! What am I supposed to do now? Can't think... too much going on... press the brakes... the brakes...." And as a big tree bounded forward to meet the rear of the now angry automobile, "PRESS THE BRAKES!!!"

The car jerked to a halt, two inches away from the oak tree.

"Whew!" Covered in sweat. Fat globules of it. "Maybe I should pack this in for today?"

You think?

"Nah, I'll get better."

And so, with another deep steadying breath, the young driver was off to the races. And did quite well, all things considered, for exactly thirty-seven seconds.

"Are you all right?" The burly police officer leaned forward in his chair, looking with concern at the youth he had just booked for driving without a license. "You feelin' dizzy?" Then, as he could more clearly see the youth's facial expression, he sat back relieved, his chair wheezing uncomfortably under his weight. The kid was just scared.

The cop regarded the new criminal with an odd mixture of sympathy, annoyance, and boredom, as the youth reached upwards, unconsciously gnawing already bitten-down cuticles. He'd seen it all before. Made you just wanna grab 'em and shake 'em, shake 'em until their teeth rattled. He sighed, suddenly losing his anger.

"Little late for them crocodile tears now, huh? What on earth were you thinking?"

"I don't know, sir. I'm just a young driver."

"Let's see. You drove a motor vehicle without a license, coached by a checklist you got off the internet. Oh, and let's not forget the advanced driving tips from your best friend — Chuck — whom I booked last week for running a red light.

"You 'drove' barely fifty yards before crashing into a telephone pole, gashing open your own forehead. And you call yourself a driver?"

The usual head hanging. "No, sir. Just a young motorist."

The officer looked incredulously at the kid. "Have you ever heard of a young road?"

"No."

"An inexperienced Lexus?"

"No."

"How many young stitches in that gash of yours?"

A sullen glare. "Eight."

"What makes you think there is such a thing as a young motorist?"

Suddenly all bravado deflated. "My dad's gonna kill me."

"No, he won't. But that's just because I ain't your daddy."

The officer rose wearily to his feet. "Here's your ticket. Drive safe, once you've learned. I think we're finished here."

The big cop left the room, leaving a subdued youth with a choice: to become a driver or stay a "young motorist."

A simple choice, really.

BODY, SOUL, AND SPIRIT

I f the spirit and soul are essentially the same, and you live your life as such, you lose nothing.

On the other hand, if you live as if no difference exists between the two and one actually does, you have done yourself a disservice. You become a person born with two arms that is only aware of—and, therefore, only uses—one: a one-handed fighter in a two-fisted fight.

You are not using a large slice of what makes you human, and you are paying for it.

But we'll get to the spirit/soul bits in a minute; we need to take care of some boring business first. A man is the sum total of his parts. This book cannot be fully understood until we know what we're made of.

The body is the tangible part of our person. We relate to our bodies with the five basic senses: sight, taste, touch, hearing, and, for better or worse, smell. The word "body" also is sometimes used to describe the whole person, especially in compound words: somebody, anybody, and so on.

The soul, much like the body, can be used to denote the whole human being, but the soul is much more commonly described as being the intangible part of humans. This embodies emotions, intellect and drive; in other words, all those parts we recognize to be part of the human experience that literally cannot be quantified by the five senses. This soul definition actually is indistinguishable from the medical definition of the mind.

Emotions live in the limbic system of the brain. In everyday language, this is called the heart, a quaint throwback to a time when it was believed that the physical heart was the container of all feelings, since it responds so eloquently to a change in emotion. That was back in the day, before we knew about neurotransmitters and hormones. The "heart" also is sometimes used to denote the whole mind.

Intellect usually is referred to in everyday language as the mind. It is understood to be part of a learning and retrieval system in the grey matter of the cerebral cortex, with memories chaired by a gnarled old gnome called the hippocampus. The hippocampus decides what information is stored in the brain and what is thrown away, the pompous old goat. He's got a powerful monopoly going on in my own brain.

Emotions and intellect are receptive in nature, in that they primarily collect and analyze both conscious and subconscious pieces of information.

Drive, on the other hand, is the will, or the expressive part of the soul or medical mind. This is the part that chooses to act, based on what has been learned or felt. In other words, will is output, to the heart and mind's input.

The spirit also has been described as the intangible part of humans. However, unlike the soul and body, the spirit is not used loosely to denote the whole person. It is always described as just a part of the total human package.

Dictionaries tend to use "spirit" and "soul" somewhat interchangeably, though the emotional aspects of our person seem to get more play with the definitions of soul, while the spirit seems to be more associated with drive. Hence both are sometimes used to denote the same things—a "mean soul," for example, or "mean-spirited" — and at other times, not — a "spirited performance" versus a "soulful performance."

Scripturally speaking, the Holy Bible consistently uses soul and body with much the same language and latitude as in secular culture.

All the souls of the house of Jacob which came into Egypt, were threescore and ten. Genesis 46:27.

Your whole spirit, soul and body. 1 Thessalonians 5:23.

Vexed his righteous soul from day to day. 2 Peter 2:8.

However, the spirit in Holy Scripture is given a much broader meaning than the secular dictionary meaning would suggest. Not different, just including more.

It is the spirit that quickeneth... the words that I speak unto you they are spirit, and they are life. John 6:63.

The spirit is defined as the life-giving part, or "life spark," of the individual.

And here is where we officially step off the ship of boring definitions. You really didn't think I wrote this book to define a bunch of old words, did you? Let's have some fun and reason together, stepping into a great debate. I may just be splitting hairs, or I may be changing lives; I'll let you decide.

A car without a driver is just a lump of inanimate junk. The driver turns that worthless piece of junk into a beautiful, growling land animal, politely dashing about the neighborhood.

But what's a driver made up of? A person, with a proper set of driving instructions tattooed on his brain. Take away the proper driving instructions, and you get: a young motorist.

Get all the driving instructions together, bind them up in a neat little manual at your local copy shop, and smack that trusty manual in the middle of the driver's seat of your vehicle. Wait for the little book to start up that gleaming automobile of yours and drive itself down your driveway. It's a safe bet to assume you'll be waiting awhile.

I think it is fair to say that, in the world of drivers/motorists, your perfect car with its perfect instructions is useless, unless you are sitting in it. The instructions need you to make driving real.

Life's best lessons are taught in parables.

The car is *the body*.
The instructions are *the spirit*.
And you, perched up in the driver's seat, are *the soul*.

The spirit and the soul need each other for the spirit to fulfill its function. The spirit "tattoos" the soul with instructions, giving it life and purpose. Good instructions create a driver. Bad, inadequate, or misleading instructions create a young motorist.

The nature of the spirit easily is seen by the success or failure of the activity it drives. It is easy to know who got proper driving instructions and who didn't, based on how they drive. Outcomes are called spiritual fruits. They do not require any special training to be recognized, and are pretty easy to measure. In other words, *anybody* can see your fruits.

Ye shall know them by their fruits. Do men gather grapes of thorns, or figs of thistles? Matthew 7:17.

Even a child is known by his doings, whether his work be pure, and whether it be right. Proverbs 20:11.

Let's demonstrate the unique spirit/soul relationship using a musical example.

The word "guitarist" implies three things: a person, a guitar, and knowledge of how to play the instrument. Remove the knowledge, and you are left with a person holding a guitar, creating a symphony of discordant notes. Take away the person, and you have a guitar with a set of playing instructions, and no sound whatsoever.

It would appear the quality of music you produce depends on the nature of the musical instruction you received. But you also need to show up, for any music to be played at all.

Hey, soul man, you bad boy, you. You always in the driver's seat, bad boy, you. You better learn to drive, you bad boy, you.

Famous lyrics suddenly make much more sense, right? Please, don't say, "Yes." I just made them up.

The soul is of extreme importance. It is not a dirty, shameful thing, as sometimes depicted, nor is it an idol to be worshipped. It houses the mind in its entirety—the emotional, analytical, and expressive—and is central to all true expressions of humanity.

Keep thy heart, with all diligence, for out of it are the issues of life. Proverbs 4:23.

Is that it, then? What it means to be human? In other words, is the spirit just contextual instruction to the soul, which in turn cranks up the body to do crazy stuff? Could my cat—with the right instructions, of course—become human, and dance like Usher?

The spirit contains instruction, and you are *never wrong* when you say the spirit gives instructions to any purpose-driven system. However, a certain type of spirit is required to plug into a corresponding soul, just like a certain type of key only works in a specific locking device. I do not have full knowledge of the human spirit, but there is irrefutable evidence of its existence and effects—or, to use your newly learned Christian-Speak 101, spiritual fruits. Animals possess a spirit, but it is very different from the human one.

Let's do a mental exercise together. Think of yourself or some other person, if you prefer—on second thoughts, maybe you should limit this exercise to yourself, as it's safer—totally divested of every stitch of clothing, makeup, combs, brushes, cream, pomade or any of the things we typically use to dolly ourselves up.

Imagine yourself, in your birthday suit, lined up with other animals in the world. As many creatures as you can think of. Evaluate yourself in comparison to them.

You are not the largest.
You are not the smallest.
You are not the fattest.
You are not the skinniest.
You are not the fastest.
You are not the slowest.
You are not the ugliest.
You are certainly not the most beautiful.
You are not the most fragile.
You are not the hardiest.
You are not the strongest.
You are not the weakest.
You are not the most flamboyant.
You are not the most lackluster.
You are not the only creature to walk on two legs.

You are not the least intelligent.
You are not the most intelligent.

And, despite your texting prowess, you are probably not the best creature at using opposing thumbs.

So, what are you, exactly? The word you are searching for, in terms of talents and natural abilities, is *mediocre*.

The fact that I still walk the planet earth makes me, officially, a freak of nature.

Drop me off at the North Pole, and I freeze to death. Put me at the equator, and I fry to death. Drop me in the sea, and I drown. Put me in the desert, and I die of dehydration before my chubby legs can get me to the next oasis. And if I actually make it to the oasis, I die of dysentery, drinking the water.

According to every logical measure we can think of, humans should not dominate the planet. In fact, based on not really having a unique intrinsic talent, we should be at best an endangered species, and at worst, extinct. Instead, we have figured out how to

- Farm;
- Build;
- Manipulate our world to such an extent that we travel thousands of miles in a few hours;
- Make huge cold storage plants for healthy food to be kept and eaten for years;
- Invent startling surgical and medical techniques;
- Make — and break — the stock market;
- Build houses higher than the tallest trees;
- Walk on the moon;
- Send other creatures to the moon;
- And create entertainment by having animals twenty times our size sit their hindquarters on stools.

Who the heck is man, anyway? Believe me, I'm not the first one to ask that question.

What is man, that thou art mindful of him? Or the son of man, that thou visitest him? Psalm 8:4.

The difference is that mysterious intangible part, the part that makes possible the seemingly impossible: the human spirit.

The human spirit is the gap between who you logically should be and who you actually are.

This is a functional definition of the spirit that, at least to me, is much more easily understood. It actually demonstrates a rarely used type of thinking I've dubbed "subtractive thought." But we'll get to that later.

Removing the spirit removes contextual instruction, among other things. You are left with an absolute lack of reason, a mirror of the crudest part of animals or, in other words, a brute. You are no longer human, for there is no such thing as a spiritless human.

Whoso loveth instruction loveth knowledge: but he that hateth reproof is brutish. Proverbs 12:1

Take fast hold of instruction; let her not go: keep her; for she is thy life. Proverbs 4:13.

In conclusion, there is a spirit in every person. It contains and gives instructions. It, therefore, creates life as we know it. We can define it by subtractive thought, and we'll get to know it even better by adding information to what we already know of it, as we go along.

A man is indeed the sum total of his parts: body, soul, and spirit.

LAST WORDS

So, do animals have spirits? For a long time I believed that they didn't, but I have come to the belief that the preponderance of biblical evidence suggests that they do.

My first indication that animals may have spirits came one day when I bumped into a verse in the Book of Ecclesiastes.

Who knoweth the spirit of man that goeth upward, and the spirit of the beast that goeth downward to the earth? Ecclesiastes 3:21.

This got me thinking: I thought about Elijah being taken up to heaven in chariots of fire carried by fiery horses. I thought of Jesus in the Book of Revelation riding on a white horse in heaven. I considered Balaam's donkey seeing an angel, a spirit not visible to Balaam the prophet himself.

Non-spiritual beings should not be located in spiritual places, nor should they perceive spiritual beings.

Besides, we now know that measured effect is just a fancy phrase for spiritual fruits. I spied my neighbor's dog having a "measured effect" on my front lawn the other day, as his owner benevolently watched.

Naughty spirit.

THE ROCK

❖

P *uuussssh!!!*
   The three men pushed with everything they had, neck veins bulging, sweat coursing down muscular backs, as they tried to move the large boulder. But the rock would not move. This was particularly frustrating, as they were not small men.

These were three big, husky fellows, men who worked in a quarry, accustomed to hard physical work and having their way with rocks—with the right machinery, of course. But there were no wrecker balls and no bulldozers out here.

Just a big fat rock, barely a hundred yards from the "Falling Rocks" sign, sitting in the middle of the road, as if punched off a cliff by a giant's heavy fist.

The steep hill made getting around the offending boulder a dangerously tricky proposition, at best. The current stretch of road had no cell phone reception on account of the hills. I guess this was the stretch not covered by the popular carrier AT&T, the missing three percent, as advertised.

But even if the phones worked, who do you call about a boulder in the road? 911? FEMA?

Oh, no. No one was waiting three days in this heat.

Besides, the boulder looked movable; it was big, but not that big. The coordinated efforts of three or four strong men probably could push it over enough to let a car through safely.

Yet their efforts were, with every passing minute, looking more foolhardy. But they had started, and testosterone had joined the party.

"I can't believe this! Seven years I've been coming up here, and I ain't never seen no fallin' rock on this road."

"Always a first time, I guess."

"You reckon? One more time. One, two, three, push!"

The day had started out well enough, with two old friends taking a new colleague out fishing. It had been a friendly gesture, but their cheeriness was fading fast.

They needed a coordinated effort to move this thing. Unfortunately, the new guy's grasp of English—to put it delicately—lacked the *sophistication* for such coordinated activity. He pushed when they paused for breath, and sucked air when they pushed. Quite frankly, he was getting on their nerves.

So, one can probably understand their irritation when another car pulled up, and a smiling young Filipino hopped out.

You could almost understand the frustration that led one "rock pusher" to say, in a muttered undertone, "What's this, a U.N. summit with no interpreters?"

"Wow! Big rock! By the way, I heard that." The new arrival pointed a playful finger at "Big Country," who could feel a warm, embarrassing flush spread up his neck, a flush that had nothing to do with the heat.

"OK, OK! Let's see if we can get this thing moving!" The Filipino, sizing up the new guy, nodded at him. *"Como se yama, mi amigo?"*

"Jose."

"Manny." They shook hands like old pals and rattled off some in rapid-fire Spanish after which Manny turned, with a toothy grin.

"OK, OK. Me and Jose will push here and here, then you and... Sorry, what's your name?"

30

"Tiny. And Colt. Or you can call him Big Country."

A surprised look. "Really? Nice to meet you. Tiny and Big Country from here and here." With that, Manny—all five foot, two inches of him—took his position, and after a dramatic three-finger countdown leaned his skinny shanks—and zero strength—into it.

And so it came to pass that three and a half men moved a boulder in two languages.

After it was all over, Tiny clapped Manny on the shoulder.

"Thanks, man. You're pretty good at coordinating stuff." Then he added mischievously, "You work in a chain gang before?"

Again, that grin. "No way, man. I'm a marketing major in college."

"Well, Manny, whatever you're sellin,' I'm buying!"

After the relieved laughter of shared experience died down, he added, "Hey, sorry about what I said earlier. I was just frustrated."

"Walang anuman, mi amigo. De nada. After all, we all get to go home now, no?"

WHO IS JESUS?

I n a brief recap, we have learned that being human means having a body, soul, and spirit.

Every spirit contains *instructions*.

Every soul contains *choice*.

Every body is the *vehicle* by which that choice is carried out.

In this chapter, we get to discuss a particular human: Jesus Christ. Let's see what secular history has to say about him.

Historically, Jesus Christ is known as a charismatic Jewish rabbi who lived and walked the earth about two thousand years ago. He had (yawn) an extensive following of predominantly Jewish people in the then Roman province of Judea.

He was deemed a political threat (more yawns), tried by the Roman authorities on counts of treason against Caesar, and sentenced to death. And then he died (gentle snore).

Sorry. History and politics wear me out. So, we have a wannabe charismatic rebel who got popped—*two thousand years ago,* no less. I don't live in Judea; I literally *ate* Caesar for lunch the other day, and the Romans? Who cares?

Stop. Rewind. Erase that. We'll start again.

WHO IS JESUS?

In this chapter, we get to discuss a very special human, as the whole idea of being a Christian rests squarely upon his shoulders. Who was—is—Jesus Christ?

I say we should take his measure. Yes, that's right. Let us literally take his measure, because measured outcomes—spiritual fruits—will tell us who he is.

Remember: Spiritual fruits do not require any special training to be recognized, and are pretty easy to measure.

In other words, anybody can measure spiritual fruits. So, let's do it.

I'll start us off with an excerpt from an exciting, crazy book I once read, called *One Nation Under Smoke: Decoding the Bible*.

"Some of the fundamentals of life that we battle with at one time or another have to do with good health, self-respect and direction. Especially direction. From erudite thinkers of ancient lore down to urban heroes of our time, this question of direction, I believe has been the primary one."

What basic principles determine the direction or "story" of a people?

Communication: This is the bedrock of technology and social development, otherwise called shared vocabulary.

Standards: These ensure that we don't rip each other's heads off while we share vocabulary.

Time: This is the incubation plate for our mistakes and growth, creating the space to learn.

Man's story, progress, civilization—whatever you want to call it—is about learned communication, according to set standards, over time. What a fiasco things become when you don't share language. And how much better things get when a smiling "Manny" comes along, and suddenly, you do.

Communication, standards, and time. Let's see how Jesus Christ stacks up in these three areas. You see, when I measure, I don't muck about. I go for the jugular, and *measure*. Either you measure up or you don't.

Communication: Vocabulary is actually the meaningful arrangement of words. Words—whether spoken, written, or symbolic—literally make the world go round. The unanimously acknowledged, most successful, most widely distributed, meaningful accumulation of words available today is without a doubt the Holy Bible.

No other book even comes close. Not Darwin's *The Origin of Species;* not the Torah; not Isaac Newton's principles of physics; not the Koran; not *The Kebra Nagast.* The Holy Bible is top dog. And what does this amazingly successful book have to say for itself? It claims unequivocally that everything in it is about *Jesus Christ.*

Standards: These are really a set of agreed-upon methods or *instructions* that govern the way we live in community. When gathered together, they constitute what we call a religion. I use this in its broadest sense; an exercise program could be your religion. The world boasts numerous religions, both old and new.

Today, who sits at the top of the religion pile? Two billion people—one third of the earth's population alive today—will willingly identify themselves as Christians, literally followers of *Jesus Christ.*

Time: The calendar system of the world today uses a particular yardstick to measure time. This yardstick is on all birth records, determines when Social Security checks are issued, and runs school systems and celebrations all over the world. Who is the yardstick?

One hundred B.C. means one hundred years Before Christ; 2010 A.D. actually stands for two thousand and ten years since the Year of our Lord. There he is again. I realize that others have changed it to B.C.E. to denote Before the Common Era, but how did they decide on the "Common Era?" *Jesus Christ.*

So, the spirit of this one man has somehow managed to permeate and influence every sphere of mankind's story. Literally everywhere you turn, there he is. He is the most communicated "word" on the planet and has the most would-be followers. And every time you write down the year, you acknowledge him.

The nature of a spirit is easily seen by the success or failure of the activity it drives.

Jesus Christ, you have been measured. You have been weighed. And you have been found worthy of further study. Because your spirit is nothing short of *awesome.*

LAST WORDS

If you've read this far and don't want to find out more about Jesus, if that is you, then put this book away right now. Your book is over. If you are content to slide back into your easy chair and your old way of thinking, it's not for you.

But don't say you never saw Jesus, because you did. You just chose to do nothing. Let's face it: It's infinitely easier to be a numbskull than to use your noggin.

For the invisible things of him from the creation of the world are clearly seen, being understood by the things that are made, even his eternal power and Godhead, so that they are without excuse. Romans 1:20.

I guess I do care about the Romans, after all.

THE BESTSELLER

T he sun hung low on the horizon, its soft yellow hue
highlighting the group of young people milling about
on the courtyard steps. Their elongated shadows created
interesting patterns, like stick insects in the evening light, as
they engaged in animated dialogue.

Alex held court, his intermittent gesticulations adding a
slightly comical backdrop to the lively conversation, one that
centered on the mysterious activities of a certain old man.

"No, I'm serious. Haven't you heard? It's the only one
he's gonna write!"

"Heard what?" Joe walked up, joining them on the front
steps.

"The old man has written a book."

A surprised look. "You're serious?"

"As a heart attack." Alex threw up his hands in mock
exasperation. "Why does everyone keep saying that? Of
course I'm serious!"

"What's it called?"

"*The Book of Life Solutions.*" Then, cheekily, "Aren't
you going to ask me what it's about?"

"Oh, don't be such a smart aleck."

Ruth shook her head amusedly at the play on words.
"Well, let's go get it. What are we waiting for? We can pool
our cash and buy a reference copy."

Alex, the news breaker, dropped another surprise: "Technically speaking, it's not for sale. The book is free to read and—get this—there's only one copy."

Simon, another member of the group, raised a skeptical brow. "A free book of life's answers? Where are you getting your info from?

"Simon, free means free. All we have to do is…"

There was a hubbub of excitement among the group as they climbed up the steps into the hallway, each processing the information about the old man, an old man who really needed no introduction. He was simply the old man, the one who knew everything.

People gladly traveled from all kinds of places to seek his wise counsel and hear his advice on a wide range of subjects, and nobody left disappointed. What the young group didn't know was that he had written the book a long time ago, before they were even born.

Why? Maybe because the wise old sage could see how chaotic his life would be if *everyone* came to him at *every minute* of *every day* to learn *everything*, and decided to pass on his information differently? His reasons were anybody's guess. But there was no doubt in any of their young minds about one thing; *The Book of Life Solutions* had to be the runaway bestseller of all time.

And it was. The old man was literally bursting with pride in his book. All questions answered, created in a beautifully eloquent writing style, setting it apart as a timeless masterpiece. From time to time, he added new information to the book, information pertaining to future life challenges. Hence, *The Book of Life Solutions* moved to its second edition, third edition, and so on.

Everyone was referred—with a huge arrow sign—to *The Book of Life Solutions*. People came, read sections of the book, and got their answers to life's problems. The fact that it was at the top of the bestseller list was a little absurd, since it was free. Maybe that's why Simon was still trying to buy it.

"I don't understand how it could be free," he'd say. "Nothing worthwhile in life is free. I question the authenticity of its content."

"Why not just try what it says? If it works, it's true. Just keep testing it out, from situation to situation."

"I don't know. I'll just have a chat with the old man, myself."

"Don't you think that's rather insulting? What are you going to ask him? 'Sir, I read your life solutions manual; is it true?'"

"Oh, be quiet! I'll think of what to say when I get there."

So, Simon ignored the arrow sign and decided to go straight to the old man, trying to disturb his peace, as it was rumored the old writer loved to putter about his garden, watering his beautiful flowers.

Unfortunately, he always seemed to have just missed the old man; he kept meeting an empty garden.

"Well, did you get your answer?"

"Not exactly. You see, it was the weirdest thing; the old man was never there! On maybe my third try, I noticed something funny."

"What was that?"

"The logo on the back of his comfy garden overalls, draped over a lounge chair. It read, in bold print, "Everything you need to know is in my book!""

There rose up a wave of spontaneous laughter.

"Nice one!"

"You got your answer, right?"

But Bertrand, another member of the group, was not amused. Possessed of a fiercely logical disposition, he had a whole different take on the situation.

"This guy won't talk to us, but writes a book. I'm supposed to believe that nonsense? What a mind job! Hey guys, I'm outta here."

Before anybody could stop him, Bertrand stormed off. If he had read the book, he might have noticed a formula, a common thread through everything written. The formula of doing things then seeing results, unlike the popularly used strategy of seeing results then doing things.

And so it went on, with controversy and questions swirling around the bestseller. But the book never had a dull moment.

Over time, the wise old man saw that there was a long line of people waiting to read the book, and everyone needed its vital information. So, he made the headlines again.

"Guess what? The old man decided to put the book on the internet!"

"Why's he advertising it? The demand is overwhelming enough as it is."

"He's not advertising it. He's made it an e-book."

"Now, that is a master stroke of genius. There are laptop computers and internet access via satellite in Antarctica, deep in the Amazon, Germany, Siberia, Myanmar, and France, the U.S. and Burkina Faso! All you have to do is Google *The Book of Life Solutions*, and, *voila*! Multiple users are reading the same e-book at the same time!"

"Sheer genius! Now why didn't I think of that myself?"

"Because you are you. You're not him."

"Okay, so I'm not him. But can someone tell me what the story is with Ben?"

"Yeah, what's up with that? He was the one who introduced us to the old man in the first place! Why does he have such a problem with the old man's book?"

Ben and his group still wanted to consult with the old man personally, so they could have bragging rights. They went to where they had heard he lived, but saw only a note on the front gate: "Gone on indefinite sabbatical to 'Graceland.' I'll be wearing my favorite overalls when I get back!"

Ben and company scratched their heads, wondering what it meant. They formed a quorum and decided to wait for the old man to return. Maybe he'd explain the note when he got back.

WHO IS JESUS?
JESUS THE SPIRIT

W̲elcome back! I'm glad you're here. I really mean
that. You're an inquisitive soul, and persistence pays
off; I know that mine has. Let's forge ahead. What have we
learned so far?

Being human means having a body, soul, and spirit.

Every spirit contains instructions.

Every soul contains choice.

Every body is the vehicle by which that choice is carried
out.

And Jesus Christ's spirit is worthy of further study, because his fruits are *awesome*.

So, let's study this awesome man's spirit. What is Jesus
Christ's spirit made of?

In the not-so-old days, before the internet, it was customary to seek an expert source of information about your
topic of interest in a place other than your bedroom. Those
were the days before we all became self-help gurus.

Now, we get all our answers from Google or the nearest
online herbal supermarket. I'm an old new kind of a guy, so
forgive my nostalgia for the good old days of libraries and
research conducted furtively, in bookstores.

But today, I have good news for both ancients and newbies: The source of information for our next topic can be found in all these places! For information on Jesus Christ's spirit, there is only one place to really go for expert advice — the Holy Bible. We'll start our search from Page One, literally the very beginning of the book.

In the beginning God created the heaven and the earth. Genesis 1:1.

The Bible contends that in the beginning, whenever that was, everything in the universe was made by God. No surprise there. This is the Bible we're talking about, after all.

So, what else does the Bible have to say about things in the beginning? We'll have to zip forward several hundred pages to find that phrase again.

In the beginning was the Word, and the Word was with God, and the Word was God. The same was in the beginning with God. All things were made by him; and without him was not anything made that was made. John 1:1-3.

That's benign enough stuff. The universe was created according to a set of *instructions.* "The Word" is just a summary term for all instructions, words spoken, written, and symbolized, all tied up in a neat little package. And if, as the Bible contends, someone made the sky, I would certainly hope that he had all of his instructions with him before he started. Fair enough?

Everything we have learned so far indicates that God's instructions created visible results. You know: stones, leafy vegetables, and fleshy humans.

Visible results are measurable. In other words, everything you can see, hear, touch, taste, or smell is a measured outcome of spiritual activity or *fruit.* I guess that makes you a fruitcake. I'm one, too. We're *godly fruitcakes,* or measured outcomes of God.

And the Word was made flesh, and dwelt among us, (and we beheld his glory, the glory as of the only begotten of the Father,) full of grace and truth. John 1:14.

John, in the above text, indicates that this Word was the *only begotten* of the Father. Literally speaking, God the Father spoke, and *"the Word" was the only thing he said.* All of the instructions God the Father has ever given were rolled into one child.

Since the gender used for the child is "he," we are looking for an "only begotten Son," as he will contain all of God's instructions. Can we find an "only begotten Son" in Scripture?

For God so loved the world, that He sent His only begotten son, that whosoever believeth in him shall not perish, but have eternal life. John 3:16.

Good, good! Our fruity thread of reasoning is still sound. It had to be a Son, if the Bible's amazing logic is to be believed at all.

So, God decided to place all his instructions inside a tangible Son. Why is that so strange, so *incredible* to some people? Intangible to tangible is the whole theme of the book, from the very beginning. Invisible things make visible things, or, put another way, doing things leads to seeing results.

That's the whole story of creation, anyway.

In the beginning God created the heaven and the earth. Genesis 1:1.

So now, like certain wise men of old, we are on the prowl to find out this Son's identity. What is his name?

And the Word was made flesh, and dwelt among us, (and we beheld his glory, the glory as of the only begotten of the Father,) full of grace and truth. John 1:14.

And of his fullness have all we received, and grace for grace. For the law was given by Moses, but grace and truth came by Jesus Christ. John 1:16-17.

Gotcha! We have a name: It is Jesus Christ!

But at this point, are we really that surprised? We already know that his spiritual fruits are *awesome*. He shapes life as we know it today. Who else could it possibly be?

According to the writings of John, we have unraveled a puzzle, and cobbled together an unusual story.

First, God begets the Word. Or, put another way, the Word comes forth out of God.

Second, the Word is the only begotten Son of God. In other words, the Word is the only Son of God that came forth out of God.

Lastly, the Word is Jesus Christ.

The Spirit of Jesus Christ is the sum total of all the instructions God the Father ever has given.

We just found Jesus Christ's spirit.

WHO IS JESUS? JESUS THE SPIRIT DEEPER STUDY

This is not a section for the fainthearted; read at your own peril. I am primarily addressing the "Christian" audience, some of who may have a problem with what is written here.

Being human means having a body, soul, and spirit.

Every spirit contains instructions.

Every soul contains choice.

Every body is the vehicle by which that choice is carried out.

Jesus Christ's spirit is worthy of further study, because his fruits are *awesome*.

And Jesus Christ's spirit is a book of all of God the Father's instructions.

Now, we are going to delve in murkier waters. How can Jesus Christ be God, and yet not know everything? This becomes clear when you understand what his spirit consists of.

God the Father thought about all creation, before it came into being. But nothing happened, until God the Father spoke his thoughts as words or *instructions*.

The Father *always* speaks the truth. True words are identical to the thoughts that lead to them. Therefore, when looking at *measured outcomes,* the Father's instructions perfectly mirror his thoughts, or God the Father's *Word* and his *mind* are indistinguishable. Jesus Christ is identical to his Father.

I and my Father are one. John 10:30.

However, *structurally,* they are two different Persons. The Father is greater, and Jesus clearly states this.

My Father is greater than I. John 14:28.

Now, here's the thing: If the Father does not speak or express a thought, it has not yet come forth as a "word." Therefore, Jesus Christ does not know it yet.

But of that day and that hour knoweth no man, no, not the angels which are in heaven, neither the Son, but the Father. Mark 13:32.

Whenever God the Father speaks, Jesus Christ's spirit gets updated, or, in a manner of speaking, he becomes another edition, of the same bestseller. These updates are revelations.

The Revelation of Jesus Christ, which God gave unto him, to shew unto his servants things which must shortly come to pass. Revelation 1:1.

For the Father loveth the Son and sheweth him all things that himself doeth, and he will shew him greater works than these, that ye may marvel. John 5:20.

Armed with this new information, Bible passages now take on stunningly new clarity and insight. Nothing was made until God spoke it into being, or gave instructions. Therefore, all things were made using the spirit of Jesus Christ.

God, who at sundry times and in divers manners spake... Hath in these last days spoken unto us by his Son, who he hath appointed heir to all things, by whom also he made the worlds. Hebrews 1:1-2.

I know: This whole concept is a paradigm shift, partly because we have a mental imagery of the "spirit" not unlike

Casper, the friendly ghost. But the spirit of Jesus Christ, I can assure you, is no Casper. *All* good instructions are actually Jesus Christ, an encyclopedia of all the life-giving instructions of God the Father.

> *All Scripture is given by inspiration of God and is profitable for doctrine, for reproof, for correction, for instruction in righteousness. 2 Timothy 3:16.*

All Scripture means *all Scripture*, the instructions of God in both the Old Testament *and* the New Testament.

The apostle Paul understood this quite clearly, though he frequently has been misinterpreted. In his letter to the Roman Christians of his day, he had this to say.

> *Say not in thine heart, Who shall ascend to heaven? (that is, to bring Christ down from above:) Or who shall descend into the deep (that is to bring up Christ again from the dead.) But what saith it? The word is nigh thee, even in thy mouth, and in thy heart: that is the word of faith, which we preach. Romans 10:6-8.*

This statement was made after Jesus Christ's life on earth. But that is not the first time such a statement had been made. It was spoken thousands of years before, by an Israeli spiritual leader called Moses.

> *For this commandment which I command thee this day... It is not in heaven, that thou shouldest say, Who shall go up for us to heaven, and bring it unto us... Neither is it beyond the sea, that thou shouldest say, Who shall go over the sea for us... But the word is very nigh unto thee, in thy mouth, and in thy heart, that thou mayest do it. Deuteronomy 30:11-14.*

Peter also mentioned the spirit of Jesus Christ being present in prophets, long before Jesus' earthly birth.

Of which salvation the prophets have enquired... Searching what, or what manner of time the Spirit of Christ which <u>was in them</u> did signify, when it testified <u>beforehand</u> the sufferings of Christ, and the glory that should follow. 1 Peter 1:10-11.

Let's consider more of Paul's writings, this time to a group of Christians in the Roman city of Corinth.

Moreover, brethren, I would not that ye should be <u>igno-rant</u>, how that all our fathers were under the cloud, and all passed through the sea; And were all baptized unto Moses in the cloud and in the sea; And did all eat the same spiritual meat; And did all drink the same spiritual drink: for they <u>drank of that spiritual Rock</u> that followed them: <u>and that Rock was Christ</u>. 1 Corinthians 10:1-4.

Do you see it? The life-preserving instructions that the Israelite population received in the wilderness after their exodus from Egypt were all part of Jesus Christ's spirit!

Jesus Christ's spirit is *every* good instruction, for God is good.

All the time. Even if this is to perform as elementary and unconscious a task as a change in body position, a task you have undoubtedly done several times today already. An inability to perform this most rudimentary of tasks leads to bed sores. Or, for some of us, sore bladders.

It's time to take a potty break, O ye wise reader; it does a body good.

LAST WORDS

Now, the true nature of Jesus Christ's spirit actually shows up in the scientific arena, if you know what to look for.

In biblical times, they lacked the measuring tools for atoms and photons, the big bang theory and the dual nature of matter. But they knew all about dust.

Dust is the smallest particle seen with the naked eye and understood by everyone. We all were created from it. Or, if dust offends your erudite sensibilities, from subatomic particles.

And the LORD God formed man of the <u>dust</u> of the ground. Genesis 2:7.

Every good gift and every perfect gift is from above, and cometh down from the <u>Father of lights</u>, with whom is no variableness, neither shadow of turning. James 1:17.

Do you really think you are teaching the Father of lights *anything* he doesn't already know when you wisely discuss light photons?

The key to life is really in how these particles are arranged or stacked up in relation to one another, creating bread, meteors, and toenails. Stacking methods require instructions. And instructions are given as *words:* the "Word" of God.

Choosing any words other than God's really means your stacking method of choice is no longer compatible with life. In layman's terms, you just jacked up your own subatomic particles.

THE DESTINATION

✠

"Come on, Hon. I'm taking you out tonight."
"Really? Where are we going?"
"Can't tell you. It's a surprise."
"What about the boys?"
What boys? Laugh. "Don't worry about them. All you need to know is that they aren't coming!"

And so, off they went. He laid his head back against the passenger seat headrest, reveling in the delicious art of guessing the unknown.

So delicious, in fact, that he heard a gentle snore, about twenty minutes later. He made sure his date, his driver to unknown destinations, hadn't dosed at the wheel. Surprisingly, she was wide awake.

"Looks like we're headed to Nashville."

"Yep." She confidently, almost cockily, changed lanes, passing a large Winnebago. He guessed she wasn't giving any clues.

Fifteen minutes later, the driving wasn't so confident. They were lost. And the home's best navigator couldn't help, because he didn't know where they were going.

"Hey, Babe, maybe you could let me know: What area of town we are headed to? You know, not exactly where, God forbid, but just the general area?"

"Well, we are headed toward Vanderbilt."

And so, on they went with a combination of spousal collaboration and a huge dollop of blind faith. Several turns later, he spied a sign toward Lipscomb University.

"Are we headed to Lipscomb University?"

"Mmm, hmm." The sunny disposition was back. Later he discovered it was a concert sponsored by Way FM 88.7. Activity suddenly accelerated to an excited blur: the slight anxiety of parking; the cold, breezy walk to the warm, welcoming foyer; the jostle of vibrant, laughing bodies; the purchase of snacks and T-shirts: the bumping into a couple of familiar faces with shouts of greetings; and voices raised over the pulsing rock music pounding in the background. Above all was the animated face of his wife, talking over the chattering din, all navigational woes totally forgotten. He smiled, love in his heart.

They arrived at their seats. But there was still one last snippet of information he needed, and he turned to her.

"So, who's playing tonight?"

"Where have you been, under a rock? It's Mercy Me and the farewell concert of Audio Adrenaline!"

"Ah."

Man, you're slow.

Adrenaline it was. The concert was a fitting tribute to a great Christian rock band that, after strings of hits spanning over a decade, decided to hang it up. There was the pulsating rock music; a hopping, waving audience; shooting streamers and light effects; the works. The boys put on a show.

And after Audio A's last hurrah, out came Mercy Me, and Bart, the lead singer, spread his arms to the pumped up crowd and belted out:

"Let me introduce myself to you. This is who I am; no more, no less."

WHO IS JESUS?
JESUS THE RABBI

B eing human means having a body, soul, and spirit.
Every spirit contains instructions.

Every soul contains choice.

Every body is the vehicle by which that choice is carried out.

Jesus Christ's spirit is worthy of further study, because his fruits are *awesome*.

Jesus Christ's spirit is a book of all of God the Father's instructions.

And Jesus Christ's spirit is every good instruction, for God is *good*.

I don't know about you, but I love these recaps. So, on to the next topic. Who is a Jewish rabbi?

A Jewish rabbi is a cross between a teacher and a leader.

The rabbi does more than just teach his students. He leads them in the now-shared experience of his own life. We could say, in a nutshell, the rabbi's creed is: Whatever I can do, you can do also.

The student is, therefore, actually an apprentice or disciple. The rabbi is more like a team leader. He teaches you his trade and *shows you who he is.*

Historically, Jesus Christ was a Jewish rabbi. Of course, we now know he was much more than that. He was in the habit of performing miracles that defy current scientific explanation, such as walking on water.

They see Jesus walking on the sea, and drawing nigh unto the ship: and they were afraid. But he saith unto them, It is I; be not afraid. John 6:19-20.

And teleportation.

Then they willingly received him into the ship: and immediately the ship was at the land whither they went. John 6:21.

What a rabbi could do, his disciples also could do. Peter, one of Jesus' apprentices, asks if he can walk on water as well—and *does.*

And when Peter was come down out of the ship, he walked on the water, to go to Jesus. Matthew 14:29.

Later on, as they gained more confidence, the disciples learned to teleport at will.

And when they were come up out of the water, the Spirit of the Lord caught away Phillip, that the eunuch saw him no more. Acts 8:39.

Welcome to rabbi school. Exciting stuff, isn't it? Let's just say the students were having the *ride* of their lives. They couldn't *wait* to go to school in the morning!

However, Jesus was much more than just an amazing rabbi. He had a strange message for the would-be apprentices of his day; not all of them could take it.

Then Jesus said to them, Verily, verily, I say unto you, Except ye eat the flesh of the Son of man, and drink his blood, ye have no life in you. John 6:53.

These were Jesus Christ's very own words, recorded in the Gospels. Unfortunately, those words lost him many disciples, who, dazzled by his miracles and charisma, were quite happy with him until he started calling them—at least to their way of thinking—to be cannibals.

The Jews therefore strove among themselves, saying, How can this man give us his flesh to eat? John 6:52.

That's when they decided he was crazy, and took off.

Many therefore of his disciples, when they heard this, said, This is an hard saying; who can hear it?... From that time many of his disciples went back, and walked no more with him. John 6:60, 66.

Jesus tried to explain that he was referring to his *spirit*, and their *spirits*. Just as our fleshly bodies require nourishment with food and drink, so do our spiritual bodies need nourishment, with the Word of God, his Father's instructions, which is the spirit of Jesus Christ.

When Jesus knew in himself that his disciples murmured at it, he said unto them, Doth this offend you?... the words that I speak to you, they are spirit, and they are life. John 6:61, 63.

Even the twelve disciples that stayed with him did not understand what he was saying until much later. It is a phenomenal testament to their faith that they still believed in him, even though they did not understand who he was. I am blown away by them, and equally tired of modern day "Christians" bashing the faith of that group of twelve, minus one.

But Jesus Christ knew it was going to take more than their faith to handle what was coming, after he was gone. They needed to know, *really know*, who he was. In fact, it was so important that Jesus Christ would not leave the earth, or even get crucified, until they got it.

I shall shew you plainly of the Father... For the Father himself loveth you, because ye have loved me, and have believed that I came out from God. I came forth from the Father, and am come into the world. John 16:25-28.

The disciples' response?

His disciples said unto him Lo, now speakest thou plainly, and speakest no proverb. Now are we sure that thou knowest all things, and needest not that any man should ask thee: By this we believe that thou camest forth from God. Jesus answered them, Do ye now believe? John 16:29-31.

Jesus almost immediately launches into a thanksgiving prayer to God the Father, a prayer which spans the whole of John 17. And in John 18? Jesus is arrested in the Garden of Gethsemane, and subsequently crucified.

So, this inner-circle group of Jesus, who had seen him feed thousands with a handful of food, heal the sick, walk on water, and, more recently, raise their buddy Lazarus from the "four-day dead," did not really understand who he was.

They knew who he said he was.
They knew what he could do.
They did what he said, with miraculous results.
But that was not enough.

None of those things captured what set him apart from all other men.

Adam is called the son of God in the Scripture.
Elisha raised a widow's dead son.
Isaiah healed the King Hezekiah.
Elijah fed a widow and her son for one year with oil from one pot.
Moses and the Israelites walked "in" water. *Close enough.*
Other religions have other miraculous stories.
Magician David Copperfield has pulled off a few "wows," too.

But Jesus being all the Father's words changed his disciples forever, for they now understood who he *really* was. This knowledge would sustain them decades later, through years of persecution and rejection, even in the face of astounding miracles and triumph. The boys finally got what it meant to be a Christian.

They also now understood that there were not "many paths to the top of Mount Fuji," though a lot of truth may be seen and identified in other people and religions.

So, did the disciples all become rabbis? More importantly, are *we* now called to be Jewish rabbis? Let's see what Jesus had to say.

The scribes and Pharisees sit in Moses' seat... but do not ye after their works: for they <u>say</u>, and <u>do not.</u> For they... love the uppermost rooms at feasts... and greetings in the *markets, and to be called of men, Rabbi, Rabbi. Matthew 23:2-7.*

But be ye not called Rabbi: for one is your Master, even Christ; and all ye are <u>brethren</u>. Matthew 23:8.

So, we are not all Jewish rabbis. Thank God, because that would require some serious lifestyle adjustments! But you are a sibling, and elder siblings teach younger ones.

My elder brother coached me in high school chemistry when I was woefully deficient in it. The result was that I made exemplary grades and lost my fear of the subject. He modeled what he knew and I learned from him. He didn't invent chemistry, but he showed me how it worked.

Like a rabbi, an elder brother is a source of on-the-job learning. Unlike the rabbi, he never claims to be the source of the knowledge. He is simply one cog in a wheel by which that knowledge is passed on, much like a foreman on a work line.

An elder sibling leads by personal example.

The beauty of this approach is that modeling the Jesus lifestyle goes with the astounding Jesus *results*. A lack of results only can mean one thing: You did not follow Jesus' instructions.

The modern church needs to have the same understanding. Put aside personal pride, and the need to be called "Rabbi!" in the streets. And please, be a brother, not a lecturer!

Lead by personal example, and examine your results. If they are not as amazing as those of Jesus, *you are not doing the right thing*. Reexamine your methods and change.

Put to rest dissenting opinions within the church organization. That goes especially for Old Testament versus New

Testament or grace versus law pundits. This is *not* what Jesus taught.

Clarify the difference between Christians and good, decent individuals who are non-Christian. Good individuals who see Jesus Christ as just one of several ways to true redemption and life are more likely to entertain the idea of following him, *if they are told who he really is!*

No wonder Jesus Christ had to make his friends, the building blocks of his church, understand him. A modern reenactment of that memorable scene from two thousand years ago would probably look like this:

JESUS CHRIST: "You guys are not just my followers, you are my friends. There is something really important you need to know about me."
DISCIPLES: "Oh, cool! What's that?"

Let me introduce myself to you.
This is who I am; no more, no less.

JESUS CHRIST: "Do you get who I am? I mean, really get who I am?"
DISCIPLES: "Wow! Now we get it!"
JESUS CHRIST: "This is important, guys. It's crucial."
DISCIPLES: "Yes, we get it."
JESUS CHRIST: "Thank God! Thank you, Father, for preparing my friends. I can go now, Dad; I can go now. Let's finish this."

LAST WORDS

Have you ever wondered what happened to Jesus' spirit when he died? Well, this is quite interesting: His spirit went right back to God the Father. It was his soul that descended into the ground.

And when Jesus had cried with a loud voice, he said, Father, into <u>thy hands</u> I commend <u>my spirit</u>. Luke 23:46.

This is what happens to *every* human being's spirit when they die. The spirit goes back to God. The body goes back to the earth.

Then shall the dust return to the earth as it was: and the spirit shall return unto God who gave it. Ecclesiastes 12:7.

But the soul, or mind, the part of you that uniquely identifies you as *you*, where does that go? That's what life's battle is really all about.

I love Ecclesiastes; it will turn all of your preconceived notions on their head. You should read it sometime.

THE STORYTELLER

⁂

"Hey, gather around; let me tell you a story." The children gathered 'round the campfire and the storyteller. They always enjoyed these impromptu tales by their camp supervisor. Some of his stories were stellar, others corny, but he was like a box of chocolates. You never knew what you might get. They all huddled closer, their fresh, eager faces silhouetted in the fire's glow.

"This is a story about Farmer Brown. Now, this story is in three distinct parts."

"Which Farmer Brown?" In every such gathering, there is always one: the "special" kid who always has something to say.

"Sshh!" "It's *a story,* Cody! Duh!" Exasperated laughter rippled through the group.

"Okay, settle down, be nice." The storyteller amusedly settled in for his story. "As I was saying, this story is in three distinct parts.

"The first part is about Farmer Brown in the kitchen. Now, Farmer Brown had a bet with his wife that he could cook dinner for their family of five. Well, there he is, clanging away with the pots and pans, to the hidden amusement of Mrs. Brown and the children. And then they all smell it, the smell of burning gravy. His daughter says, 'Dad, turn down the heat on the cooker!' A flustered Farmer Brown quickly retorts, 'Be quiet! Are you the one doing the cooking?' That's the end of part one."

The "one" pipes up again. "Bad cook, huh? He should never have taken..."

"Shush, Cody!"

"The second part is about Farmer Brown in the laundry room. Now, Farmer Brown had a bet with his elder son that he could do all the family laundry, to which Mrs. Brown almost burst out laughing aloud. So, Farmer Brown determinedly grabs a load of laundry to place in the washing machine. His younger son calls out a warning: 'Dad, don't run the colored laundry with the whites!' To which Farmer Brown answers, 'Be quiet! Are you the one doing the laundry?' That's the end of part two."

"The fourth part is about..."

Cody pounced. "Wait a minute! You said the story was in three parts!"

"Be quiet! Are you the one telling the story?" Amidst the laughter and the abashed but laughing Cody, the storyteller, a beatific smile on his face, said, "And that is the end of part three."

THE STORYTELLER
PART TWO: AIPOTU

A fter the laughing had died away, the storyteller, adjusting his glasses, said, "Let's tell a different kind of story this time. It's about a sheriff and his two sons.

"Once upon a time, the world was much smaller. So small, in fact, that it was made up of only two cities. The story is about the sheriff of Aipotu, one of the cities, nicknamed the City of Joy.

"He was a great sheriff. He had made his city a joy to all who lived in it. It was a well thought-out town, with lush greenery, beautiful homes, well-maintained streets, and paths winding through gentle hills, dotted with beautiful vineyards and orchards. There was work for all of its citizens, who were proud and happy to be in such a joyous place.

"It was commonplace to see children racing each other up and down the winding paths. Their peals of young laughter brought a smile to the faces of all who heard them. When you are truly satisfied, crime ceases to exist. This was such a town.

"Of all its citizens, though, no one appeared to enjoy it more than the sheriff's younger son. He was about your age, and didn't have a lot of responsibilities. After he had done his few household chores, he played all day long, exploring the length and breadth of Aipotu with his other young friends.

"The elder son was a grown man and a symbol of hope and pride for the town. He was an earnest, vital young man who had inherited his father's vigor, fairness, and graciousness. His energetic gracefulness made him loved in this town in a way that is difficult to describe. Privately, everyone called him the 'young king,' so regal was his bearing. He taught his young brother about responsibility, but couldn't help laughing sometimes at the youth's exuberant antics.

"One day, as the sheriff's younger boy was exploring Aipotu, he came to the border fence of the city. On the other side was a beautiful garden, with trees full of luscious-looking berries. There also was a billboard with a picture of a tall, fine-looking man in a sheriff's hat at the entrance to the garden.

"Now, he was quite hungry, but he was in a slightly awkward situation. His mouth watered for the berries, but he remembered the one strict instruction that had been hammered repeatedly into him by his dad and elder brother. He could hear their voices in his head, right now: 'Under no circumstance should you go outside the city fence. Not all places are like Aipotu.'

"*But I want the berries!* he thought. *Surely a few wouldn't hurt, especially with that nice-looking man up there on the sign to the garden. Why, he looks almost as if he is from Aipotu!* And so, before he lost his nerve, he scaled the fence, dashed into the garden, and plucked a handful of berries from a tree. He munched on them as he trotted back to the fence bordering Aipotu, the sweet, dark berry juice dripping down to his elbows and onto the front of his shorts, as he ate.

"'Why did you do it, son?'

"The sheriff's visage was incredibly sad, his heart heavy, as he gazed down at his younger son. The youth hung his head in shame, trying unsuccessfully to hide the berry stains on his shorts. That particular shade of berry juice did not exist in the city of Aipotu. The sheriff looked at the berry stains, and his heart sank.

"'I don't know, Sir. I don't know.'

"The sheriff looked with sorrow at the boy. 'Do you know what you just did? You exchanged your citizenship in Aipotu for that of the city across the fence: Kaos. It means 'City of Endless Craving.'" Heavy footfalls approached the door. The sheriff sighed.

"'Their sheriff, if he can even be called that, has come to take you to your new home. He lived in Aipotu, once, but that was a long time ago.' He was rent with sorrow looking at his boy, whose face was a literal mural of shock and bewilderment.

"The door opened, and the sheriff and his sons found themselves face-to-face with a man. He was an evil-looking man who watched the boy malevolently, an air of rot and decay about him. His eyes were unevenly spaced, and one of them seemed to be rolling off the side of his nose. His right ear seemed to have slid down, almost to the point of his chin. His teeth were broken, and his breath was foul. Yet something about his carriage looked familiar. With a jolt of recognition, the youth recoiled in horror.

"'You!' he whispered.

"The man from the billboard, hideously changed and yet strangely the same, gave a grotesque smile. He looked beyond the boy at the sheriff of Aipotu. 'The lad returns to Kaos, with me. I have full rights to this citizen. The rules are the rules. You should know; you made them.'

"The sheriff nodded sadly. 'Yes, I did.'

"The young prince was carted off by the self-proclaimed sheriff of Kaos, whose once-handsome face and body had been hideously mutilated during an ancient war. There was a sorrowful hush in the City of Joy that day."

The storyteller paused, solemnly observing his young subjects for effect. Every scrubbed young face was entranced in rapt attention.

"Now, that is just awful!"

"How terrible!"

"How sad. He should have stayed away from the berries, though."

Satisfied that he still had them hooked, the storyteller continued.

"The sheriff of Aipotu looked at his elder son, a look of total understanding passing between them.

"'You know what we have to do, don't you?'

"'Yes. I do. He can't be left in Kaos. He'll be destroyed.'

"The sheriff looked intently at his elder son, a fiery glint in his eye.

"'You know they call you the young king behind your back?'

"'Yes, Father. I know.'

"'That's because you are. You're me, all over again. The fake sheriff was right to say the rules are the rules, but you know the rules better than anybody else.' He paused.

"'You also know the sheriff of Kaos better than he knows himself.'

"Nothing more needed to be said. The two men embraced, and off went the young king to bring back his brother.

"The excitement in the city of Aipotu was palpable.

"'The young king is going to get the young master back!' A huge cheer went up, the ground vibrating with the sound, hands and arms waving, a joyous roar, wonderful to behold. It gave buoyancy to the young king as he strode out of the gate of Aipotu, into the city of Kaos.

"He walked many miles, avoiding murderers and robbers, cut off from all he had ever known. But his father's words in his ears kept him from being distracted, and love for his brother gave urgency to his steps. He ate nothing of the land, ignoring the strategically placed, delicious-looking fruit trees. Finally, he came to a huge rusty gate.

"Seemingly out of nowhere, a sack dropped over his head and strong, rough hands seized him. He heard the gate squeak open, then clang shut. He was frog-marched across a courtyard, and the sack was finally taken off his head.

"He looked around. Ranks of tortured-looking men were jogging off to one side. Others were maniacally practicing fierce hand-to-hand combat. Another group did sit-ups and pushups, agonized expressions on their faces. They all looked ragged and exhausted and yet, fiercely driven. He was in a training camp, with the members training for war: a war with Aipotu. It was the sole reason that the city of Kaos existed.

"'Ah, there you are: the young lion!' The young king turned to see the grotesque sheriff of Kaos, bent at the waist in a mocking bow, his younger brother at his side. He was shocked by the changes that already had started in the youth. His body was wasting, and he had started to have the look of crazed desperation that was characteristic of this cursed place. His eyes showed only intermittent recognition of his own brother.

"'I have come to replace my brother in Kaos city.'

"The fake sheriff laughed. 'Really?' But his mind was working at lightning speed. He knew he could turn the young pup any time he wanted; he had already proven that. But the elder brother, the heir apparent? That would deal a terrible blow to the sheriff of Aipotu, his former friend and now legendary adversary. Then he would attack, with the young king at his side. The City of Joy would be his!

"The grotesque face smiled, a terrifying thing to behold. 'Very well.' He strived to look disinterested, almost totally hiding the eager gleam in his gaze. 'He was getting kind of boring, anyway. Have it your way. He can go, but only if he wants. You can't make him leave.' He gripped the younger brother's face, inspecting it from side to side. 'I've done such a number on him already, I'm not sure he wants to leave.' He laughed, then triumphantly said, 'Free choice, remember? Another of your daddy's rules. And as you know...'

"'Yeah, yeah; the rules are the rules. Can we get on with it now?'

"And so the would-be sheriff went to work on the young king. He used all his skills: persuasion, torture, you name it, he did it.

"But the young king would not break. A long time later, the fake sheriff threw down his torture tools in disgust.

"'Why won't you break, you miserable creature? Why?'

"The young king, through his battered and bruised lips, smiled.

"'Because you are defined by two things: revenge and greed. Because you are not content in Kaos; you hate it here! Because unless I'm broken, I'm of no use to you. Because without me, you can't get what you want: Aipotu. Because my father already has what you want: Aipotu. Therefore, I have time, and you don't. I can wait you out.

"'I know you, better than you know yourself.'

"The fake sheriff looked stricken. He now understood he had been outmaneuvered, all within the framework of the rules. He loosened the young king's shackles. 'You may go. You're no use to me.'

"The young king, physically scarred, spent but triumphant, walked out of the door and into the courtyard to where his younger brother squatted, shivering, in a corner.

"'Come on, Bro. It's time to go home.' The youth looked up at him vacantly.

"Once again, he said, 'It's time to go home.' A single tear rolled down the young king's cheek. 'I can't force you, though. You have got to leave this place, like I am leaving, looking neither to the left nor right. With your eyes set on only one place: Aipotu, your home.'

"He squatted down beside him at eye level. 'All you have to do is call out, and I'll come get you. He,' he said, pointing in the general direction of the creepy man, 'can't stop me from coming to get you, after you have chosen to leave. That's also in the rule book.' He turned to the defiant but desperate-looking sheriff of Kaos.

"'The writer of the rules always knows them better than the reader of them. My spirit cannot be broken.'

"He walked to the gate. 'One last thing, little brother: After this, no more berries, right?' The youth finally seemed to hear, from the end of a long tunnel. The ghost of a tremulous, tentative smile flitted across his otherwise solemn visage.

"'Right. No more berries.'

"And with a brief, satisfied nod, the young king stepped out of Kaos."

WHO IS JESUS?
JESUS THE SAVIOR

B eing human means having a body, soul, and spirit.
Every spirit contains instructions.

Every soul contains choice.

Every body is the vehicle by which that choice is carried out.

Jesus Christ's spirit is worthy of further study, because his fruits are *awesome*.

Jesus Christ's spirit is a book of all of God the Father's instructions.

Jesus Christ's spirit is every good instruction, for God is *good*.

And Jesus Christ is, therefore, different from all other men.

This is the last part of this section. We are going to discuss Jesus as our Messiah, and why we need saving. But before that, let's segue for a couple of minutes to get a fresh look at a quantity we are all quite familiar with: time. Why? Because we are going to need this perspective in order to understand salvation.

God operates both in and out of time. God created time. This means that God had to exist before time was created. God, therefore, knows the full span of time: when it began and when it ends.

Time is for fixing "stuff." Why create time in the first place? Earlier on, I described time as the incubation plate for our mistakes and growth. I can't say I fully understand it, but I do know that time gives us an opportunity to do things over. Knowing everything does not necessarily translate to doing everything correctly. For example, I am yet to find the human being who contends that exercise is evil. Yet, how many times have you exercised this week?

Without time, consequences would be immediate, with no hope of redemption. Every willful bad choice would lead to immediate death. Methinks a time continuum to learn about God is much better. And from God's point of view, he knows just how much "crazy stuff" I'm capable of, over time.

Now, let's get down to the business of salvation.

I had an interesting chat with an exciting, insightful man the other day. He gave me a fresh perspective on God's plan for our lives, here on earth.

God is working to bring man from a post-fall reality to a pre-fall inheritance.

Man was made perfect and in God's image. This meant he was endowed with the God-characteristic of free will.

Now here's an interesting thought: God knows everything, every permutation of every set of actions, and all resultant outcomes. He knows evil and all possible expressions of it, from the seemingly innocent, to the most offensively depraved. Yet God limits himself to doing good things — despite free choice.

Let no man say when he is tempted, I am tempted of God: for God cannot be tempted with evil, neither tempteth he any man. James 1:13.

He lives by his own rules, understanding that all sins, no matter how innocuous-looking, end in the same place: death.

And sin, when it is finished, bringeth forth <u>death</u>. James 1:15.

The wages of sin is <u>death</u>. Romans 6:23.

So, how did death get here? Let's look at an interesting, if somewhat familiar, Bible story.

After God made the first two people, he put them in a beautiful, lush garden he had made for them called the Garden of Eden. They were appointed as gardeners and custodians of this utopian paradise, with food provided in all kinds of abundance from the produce of the garden.

This was the quintessential package deal—work from home and get paid at home, a fully functional health insurance policy, paid vacation, touring from one side of Eden's garden to the other. And this garden was *huge*. All on one condition: Stay away from a particular tree. Just one tree.

And the LORD God commanded the man, saying, Of every tree of the garden thou mayest freely eat: But of the tree of the knowledge of good and evil thou shalt not eat of it: for in the day that thou eatest thereof thou shalt surely die. Genesis 2:16-17.

Well, both the first man and woman ate of the fruit, believing that being alive and knowing God would nullify the truth of God's instructions: Jesus Christ, the spirit. They had been tricked by God's old adversary, Satan. It was the first time Satan had used that trick on a living soul: *You are a living soul; you are perfect! You can do no wrong!*

It worked.

On that day, the man and woman both lost their connection to God's blueprint for life, and died. The instant that little fruit-eating antic occurred, God's firstborn Son, Jesus Christ, was destined to be offered up in man's place. For the love of the Father, and the love of the firstborn Son.

For God so loved the world, that he gave his <u>only begotten son</u>, that whosoever believeth in him should not perish, but have everlasting life. John 3:16.

I live by the faith of the Son of God, who loved me, and gave himself for me. Galatians 2:20.

Adam was supposed to grow into his heritage over a period of time. And Adam was clipping along quite nicely, until he and his wife willfully sinned against God. Adam had done the work of sin; sin's paycheck is death; and therefore, his paycheck of death was made ready. But God sent Jesus to collect that paycheck in Adam's place.

How was such a replacement possible? To better grasp this, we are going to have to understand where Jesus went when he died. Just for a minute, we're all going to take a trip to a place called hell.

Hell is a place where the souls of people who are no longer spiritually connected to God go. As we learned earlier, death is a lack of spiritual connection to God, who is life itself.

God turned away, for a time, from his firstborn Son. This, far beyond the physical beating, cut Jesus Christ to the quick. That was the precise moment when the Son of God died. The agony of rejection made him burst out with his first pain-filled words, on the cross.

My God, my God, why hast thou forsaken me? Mark 15:34.

Jesus had been through all kinds of trials, during his life on earth. There was extreme temptation.

And Jesus being full of the Holy Ghost returned from Jordan, and was led by the Spirit into the wilderness, Being forty days tempted of the devil. Luke 4:1-2.

There was torture, physical mutilation, and a brutal beating.

And they clothed him with purple, and platted a crown of thorns, and put it about his head... And they smote him on the head with a reed, and did spit upon him... and led him out to crucify him. Mark 15:17-20.

Ultimately, there was crucifixion. *None* of those terrible events elicited a pain-filled response like that.

At that point, Jesus knew he was dead. He said it was finished and voluntarily released his spirit to the Father who gave it. His soul descended to where all souls had to go when disconnected from the spirit of God the Father: He went to hell.

However, God the Father and Jesus Christ knew the rules better than Satan did. Let's look closely at Paul's statement, once again.

The wages of sin is <u>death</u>. Romans 6:23.

Death is both a spiritual being and a state of existence. Death grabs people and pops them in hell. That is his threat or *sting*, because when you see him, *you know where you're headed.*

Death—as a state of existence—is a wage or a *paycheck*. And if death is a wage, then sin must be some kind of work. Jesus did not do the work of sin. Therefore, he did not deserve to be paid its wages.

A soul that did not earn its way to hell could not eternally reside there. Jesus did not belong in hell, as death is earned by sin—willfully disobeying God's instructions or, put another way, departing from a blueprint compatible with life. Hell had to let him go.

Hell was created by God, for those who had *earned it*.

That's how Jesus went to hell with something other than a one-way ticket.

How much of a price did Jesus pay for our sin? It is literally unfathomable. God loved man so much; he did not want him to die. So, looking through the whole time continuum, God tallied the total amount of sin that Adam—and, through him, his descendants would create, all the way through to the end of time—and how much in "death wages" they had earned.

God then summoned Satan and Hades and said, "I'll pay you for Adam's paycheck." Satan and Hades agreed to the deal.

However, Adam *did the sin work*. Technically speaking, unless he agrees to the brokered deal between God and Satan, Adam and all his descendants get to keep his originally earned paycheck: *death*.

Why death to Adam and his descendants, and not just the first two humans? I honestly don't know.

Maybe Adam's eating of the forbidden fruit caused a genetic malformation of some sort, passed down by him through all human DNA: one that is lethal to the spirit, once it is incorporated into the person that becomes you or I, as a newly formed zygote or embryo. Sort of like the newly formed flesh, with its lethal genetic information, now becomes a cyanide gas chamber for the spirit. Or, when he ate the fruit, he killed all predetermined spirits that were to come on earth as men and women, in one fell swoop. Who knows?

Whatever the reason, Adam was in trouble, the deal of a lifetime was on and Satan was gambling big money, because from his standpoint, the potential dividends were huge. What could those anticipated dividends possibly be? Brace yourself, for you are about to learn a hidden truth: Satan's dream for himself.

Satan really didn't give a toss about Adam, his descendants, or even Jesus Christ, the Son of man. From the devil's standpoint, people are just pawns in a deadly chess game, a means to an end. So, what does Satan really, *really* want?

He wants to rule all creation from heaven, like God the Father himself.

Satan's dream is ruling the *kingdom of heaven*. The Book of Isaiah outlines Satan's dream.

How art thou fallen from heaven, O Lucifer, son of the morning... For thou hast said in thine heart, I will ascend into heaven... I will ascend above the heights of the clouds; I will be like the most High. Isaiah 14:12-15.

Lucifer was Satan's name—before he fell. You know how you feel when you wake up to a perfect, bright, sunshiny morning? That was how you felt when you gazed upon Lucifer, "son of the morning," before greed ruined him.

So, now we know Satan's motivation. But let us look closely at the things Satan wanted. They are the things promised to Jesus Christ and his brethren, mankind.

What is man, that thou art mindful of him?... Thou crownedst him with glory and honour... Thou has put all things in subjection under his feet. Hebrews 2:6-8.

But we see Jesus... crowned with glory and honour... for both he that sanctifieth and they who are sanctified are all of one: for which cause he is not ashamed to call them brethren. Hebrews 2:9,11.

Satan wants what Jesus Christ and humans have been promised: He wants to inherit the kingdom of God. If Jesus commits sin, then he has earned himself death wages; but more importantly, a new employer or master: Satan himself.

Whatever a servant owns is actually his *master's*.

The only downside for the devil was, unless Christ sinned himself or died, he was of no use to Satan. He already knew who Jesus Christ really was. Satan had no real interest in the goings on of a dark, hot, ugly place called hell; he is looking for a bargaining chip to somewhere much, much *nicer*.

Since Satan already owned Adam, he would now totally own mankind's entire inheritance. Satan would get his dream: the kingdom of God. As I told you: The stakes were high.

But Jesus had committed no sin through all that torture and temptation. Satan recognized that Christ's indomitable spirit could not be broken. After all, the devil is also a creature of creation, and he has to play by the rules.

Knowing that Christ being raised from the death dieth no more; death hath no more dominion over him. Romans 6:9.

So, our Lord and Savior rose from the dead on the third day, after descending into the bowels of the earth. Gleefully clasped in his right hand was an invoice, titled *Mankind's Death*, with a "paid-in-full" stamp on it.

Thus it is written, and thus it behooved Christ to suffer, and to rise from the dead the third day. Luke 24:46.

O death, where is thy sting? 1 Corinthians 15:55.

But do not forget one important point. It's a crucial point because, though Jesus had triumphed on his end of the deal, there is one inescapable fact that mankind still has to deal with.

Adam did the sin work.

This is why, though mankind's wages already have been purchased, every person must of their own free will sign the deal *in their own hand, with their own signature,* to live. Once signed, that person becomes owned by and obedient to a new master: Jesus Christ. Which is quite all right, because that was mankind's pre-fall inheritance in the first place.

This is what it really means to be a Christian.

As we can see, the whole Christian system is based on the free choice principle. This principle does not change. It is a choice for each and every individual to make: Choose to leave a post-fall reality, to achieve a pre-fall inheritance.

Man's elder Brother, Savior, and King is Jesus Christ. Man has to choose Christ as the only sure way back to the wonderful kingdom he unknowingly, but willfully, abandoned.

Hence, we use Christ's blueprint to get home and call on him for help, to step our way out of "Kaos." It certainly helps that he is all the words God the Father has ever spoken. God's words lead to *life*. This is where we want to be.

I am the way, the truth, and the life: no man cometh unto the Father, but by me. John 14:6.

It certainly makes the statement easier to understand, doesn't it? It also puts a whole new spin on Jesus' response to Satan's "stone-bread" temptation.

It is written, Man shall not live by bread alone, but by every word that proceedeth out of the mouth of God. Matthew 4:4.

Translation: Man shall not live by bread alone, but by *me*.

LAST WORDS

So, is hell the same thing as Hades?

Hell is the land of the dead. However, Hades is actually the Greek mythological god of the land of the dead. Jesus uses both terms, even when addressing a Jewish audience.

One thing I do know, beyond a shadow of a doubt. Jesus would not use a word that was a fake myth to represent anything. He is aware of the origins of the word Hades.

Hades is the name of the gatekeeper to the land of the dead, and the name is sometimes extended to represent his domain—hell—with him in it. Death sends you to hell; Hades keeps you there.

Both fellows get tossed into the mother of all bonfires at the end of all time.

Good riddance.

SPIRIT LESSONS (so far...)

Being human means having a body, soul, and spirit.

Every spirit contains instructions.

Every soul contains choice.

Every body is the vehicle by which that choice is carried out.

Jesus Christ's spirit is a book of all of God the Father's instructions.

Jesus Christ is, therefore, different from all other men.

Through him, paradise lost was found.

SECTION II

THE TEAM

✠

"I'm going to die today."

It's funny how time speeds up when you are running out of it but slows down when you have none left.

He remembered once running late for work, trying to make a fifteen-minute journey in five—so intent on getting to his destination—not noticing that he was running a red light.

He recalled with vivid clarity the semi, twenty tons of unyielding steel, bearing down on him, desperately blaring its horn. Time slowed to a crawl that day, in the final desperate moments before impact. For the first time in a long time, he had time: Time enough to remember, with a sliver of regret, that he had forgotten to move the ground beef from freezer to fridge, in preparation for that evening's chili dinner.

And suddenly, it was over, death averted as the semi rushed by, missing his car by inches, leaving him shaky and weak as a kitten. He remembered a strange sensation, an odd, bitter taste in his mouth, as if his salivary glands had temporarily produced bile. Who knows? Maybe they had.

He'd cheated death that day. But today, as he slowly sank to the floor clutching his chest, his half-eaten cheeseburger and fries still sitting on the cafeteria table above him, time slowing in a now-familiar pattern, he could have sworn he heard death say, "There you are, my old friend. I've been looking for you."

Across the room, a small group of three pushed back their chairs, about to get back to the grind of the afternoon clinic. "Lunch can't last forever, though I gotta tell you, today I wish it would." The nurse smiled at the remarks from her boss. Doc was always working, but everyone who'd ever worked with him knew he wouldn't have it any other way. He was a workaholic.

They had just packed up the detritus of their lunch sandwiches when the office manager, who had absentmindedly glanced across the room, urgently tugged at the doctor's ward coat. "Doc, that guy's in trouble!"

The doctor, turning in the direction of her frantic gaze, saw the man. He was probably in his early forties, sitting on the floor with his hands clutched over his lower chest, sweating profusely, and looking straight at him. For a long moment, he was transfixed by the man's eyes, huge orbs of abject terror.

Then the years of practice kicked in.

"Go get the crash cart, quick!" The company outpatient clinic and crash cart were across the courtyard from the cafeteria, less than thirty seconds away. The nurse was off like a shot.

To the office manager: "Call 911!" As he quickly moved toward the man, he was methodically going through a checklist of potential causes.

Not choking, he's breathing. He mentally flicked away foreign-body lung aspiration, with a finger.

Still conscious. As he reached the victim, he whipped out his stethoscope.

"Sir, if you can hear me, please nod your head." The sweating man nodded as the doctor reached for his carotid pulse, simultaneously counting the rise and fall of his chest for his respiratory rate. A quick check for any diabetic, epilepsy, or allergy bracelets.

None.

"I'm just going to get your name here. Relax and don't try to speak, Sir." The doctor reached for the sick man's back pocket and flipped out his wallet: *Alfred Dwayne Walker.* "Dwayne, I'm going to listen to your chest now. Don't try to speak; we've got you."

Dwayne's chest sounded terrible. The nurse had returned with the crash cart. "Dwayne, are you allergic to aspirin?" A negative shake of the head. The doctor nodded at his nurse. Almost magically, Nurse Tina produced a chewable aspirin from the cart.

"Here, Dwayne, chew this; it's aspirin. It'll make you better." She quickly but gently fed the aspirin pill between the sick man's lips, and with satisfaction watched him chew it as she placed a blood pressure cuff on his upper arm.

A raspy croak. "Doc, what's *happening* to me?"

Tina placed an intravenous access in his opposite forearm.

The doctor placed a calming hand on his shoulder. "It looks like you're having a heart attack." Then in a clammy sweat, the squeezing, choking pain increasing to an intensity Dwayne Walker had never before thought possible, his gaze started to glaze over. As he slipped out of consciousness, he heard the doctor's voice, measured but with an unmistakable streak of urgency.

"Lay him flat! He's crashing! Come on, Dwayne, stay with me." And then a few moments later, from the end of a long, dark tunnel: "1mg of epinephrine I.V. now. What time is it?" Tina's voice floated back. "Epi on board, Doc, at 1:03 p.m. Blood pressure 81/39mmHg...." Then the swirling black clouds thickened, sucking him into an abyss of nothingness.

And so, the battle for Dwayne's life raged on as the medications permeated his being, and he was locked in a life-and-death struggle with his accomplished adversary.

"What time is it?"

He sat up in bed suddenly, with the words echoing in his head. He was in a bright room with slatted windows and a slightly antiseptic smell. It was an unfamiliar room, which he soon realized was in a hospital.

Suddenly the horror of the memories came flooding back, mixed with an equal amount of another, much more pleasant emotion: relief. He was still alive. He was still standing.

The door opened, revealing a couple of nurses and a young man in a doctor's ward coat.

"Good morning, Dwayne. I'm Dr. Ramirez, but you can call me Dr. Ram; everyone else does around here. Welcome back. You had us worried there for a minute."

Somewhat groggily: "Mornin,' Doc. How long was I out?"

"Three days." Dr. Ram blew out, through puffed cheeks. "You're a blessed man. Someone was looking out for you up there." He pointed in the general direction of the ceiling bulb.

"You had a heart attack, presenting with a very serious complication called cardiogenic shock. You're doing really well, but you're not totally out of the woods yet. You must have had one helluva team resuscitating you..."

As Dr. Ram continued to speak reassuringly, Dwayne thought about his brushes with death, and mentally took stock of his life. He did not like what he saw. In that moment, he decided, it was time to make a change. Starting now.

"Dr. Ram?"

"Yes?" Somewhat startled, Dr. Ram stopped in mid-sentence, interrupting his monologue.

"Hello." He stuck out a hand, a rejuvenated smile on his face. "I'm making a fresh start. My name's Alfred Dwayne Walker. I go by Fred, these days."

Dr. Ram looked thoughtfully at his patient. Then a slow smile of understanding spread over his face, and he clasped the outstretched hand. New name, new destiny. So be it.

"Fair enough. Good morning, Fred."

THE KINGDOM OF GOD AND THE CONCEPT OF THREES

卐

I t's time for another spiritual growth spurt.
Earlier on, we said that a spirit is the container of all instructions. We also said a certain type of spirit is required to plug into a corresponding soul, just like a certain type of key only works in a matching keyhole. The next spiritual concept to add to our knowledge list is that of spiritual mingling.

Spirits can mingle or mix with each other.

Good or bad instructions can be added to pre-existing ones; therefore, instructions contained in one spirit can be poured into another.

However, as we already know, a good or bad instruction is measured by its outcome, or spiritual fruit. Some outcomes are absolute; ninety-nine percent normal and one percent cyanide-laced food, for example, will not cut it if life is the desired outcome. I guarantee you: Eating that meal will ensure that you do not finish this book. Or another example: Instructions to walk forward and backwards cannot both be carried out at exactly the same time.

Therefore, depending on the desired outcome, some spirits cannot be mixed.

Understanding this helps us grasp the absolute position of this next member of the God unit to be introduced. He is called the Holy Spirit.

The Holy Spirit delivers life.

The Holy Spirit is the activator of all life systems, wherever they exist. He is one hundred percent life and is frequently represented symbolically in Holy Scripture as living water. Water is required by all life forms for existence, and is a tangible reminder of this member of the Holy Trinity. Remember that, the next time you have a cool drink of water!

However, we know that life is embodied by the spirit of Jesus Christ, God the Father's blueprint and manual for all life.

The Holy Spirit delivers God's Word to all creation.

He takes the words of God the Father, and makes them happen. I like to describe the Holy Spirit as working like the internet, delivering email messages of truth from the Father's web address to multiple email addresses (www. you, www.me, etc.)@thesametime.dom (for kingdom). That description probably won't fly from most pulpits, but it sure works for me.

With this understanding, let us examine what we know about how things are in heaven. Heaven and earth function on a premise of threes and thirds. This concept is so pervasive and powerful that it has to be written about.

There is God the Father, God the Son, and God the Holy Spirit. All three have the same outcome; therefore, *all three are God*.

Now, let's intricately examine a portion of the most popular prayer in the Holy Bible, the Lord's Prayer.

Our Father which art in heaven, Hallowed be thy Name.
Thy kingdom come. Matthew 6:9-10.

A kingdom usually is an area which is presided over by an ultimate authority or king.

About a thousand years ago, kingdoms were structurally two-dimensional. A kingdom was an area of land, demarcated by walls, gates, fences, etc. Within this area all people, animals, and resources were the property of the king. They served implicitly at his pleasure. Anyone who came in from outside the kingdom was subject to the king's rules, while within the kingdom.

Today, we still have some kingdoms. But there has been a subtle change in defining a kingdom's boundaries. They have become structurally three-dimensional, due to the discovery of air travel.

Now we have "kingdom airspace," which was not an issue before the advent of the airplane. If anyone flies into the airspace over a kingdom, they are warned off sternly. If that person persists in flying within the said airspace, he or she is escorted down, sometimes nicely, and at other times, not so nicely. And we'll leave it at that.

So, today, in terms of *structure*, to all intents and purposes, the kingdom area is now more accurately described as a volume. However, *functionally*, the definition of a kingdom has not changed.

A kingdom is any place the will of its king is fully expressed.

This understanding unlocks the meaning of the phrase "the kingdom of God."

The kingdom of God, therefore, is any place the will of God is fully expressed.

Always think *function* when you see the kingdom of God used in Scripture, not *form* or *structure*. In other words, stop thinking of God's kingdom primarily as a place, and start thinking of it as a way of life. The emphasis should be less about its location, and more about *what you do when you're in it*.

Now, let's go back to the Lord's Prayer. Or our discussion with God, because that is what a prayer really is.

Thy kingdom come, Thy will be done in earth, as it is in heaven. Matthew 6:10.

Jesus Christ taught us to ask for the will of God to be fully expressed here on earth. Why?

Things are supposed to work on earth as they work in heaven. Unfortunately, they don't.

Now, God made the heavens and the earth in six days and said that everything was good in the beginning. So, the key as to how things should work on earth probably can be understood by asking two questions.

First: "How do things currently work in heaven?" Second, we should ask: "How did things work on earth in the beginning—when man was first made, and everything was good?"

Things work in heaven as they always have, since it was first made. However, this does not mean stagnation.

Think of it like a computer program that hypothetically does exactly what it was made to do, with no bugs, crashes, or viruses.

It still churns out documents, databases, and spreadsheets when needed, to the delight and satisfaction of its owner. However, the program really is not being tinkered with or revised, because it is doing *exactly what it is supposed to do*. Heaven works like that.

In a manner of speaking, heaven is resting—in motion.

God the Father originates all the ideas, determines what needs to be done, and when the time is right, he speaks. As we already know, every word he speaks is the spirit of his Son, Jesus Christ.

God the Holy Spirit acts as the delivery system or enforcer, to get God the Father's Words done. In other words, the Holy Spirit brings the Word of God to all of heaven and makes it happen, with tangible results. He only does what God the Father says; no more, no less.

When he, the Spirit of truth is come, he will guide you into all truth: for he shall not speak of himself; but what-soever he shall hear. John 16:13.

But what use is cause and effect, if there is no benefi-ciary? Enter God the Son.

In the beginning he was a spirit—the Word of God—but as we know from the previous chapters, he is now a human being. As a human, he is the recipient of all things, both structural and functional. All the things God the Father's words accomplish in heaven. He is the inheritor.

God, who at sundry times and in diverse manners spake in time past unto the fathers by the prophets, Hath in these last days spoken unto us by his Son, whom he hath appointed <u>heir of all things</u>... Being made so much better

*than the angels, as he hath <u>by inheritance</u> obtained a
more excellent name than they. Hebrews 1:1-2, 4.*

**God the Father is the head. God the Holy Spirit is the
enforcer. God the Son is the inheritor.**

Hence, the Father's will is fully enacted by the collaboration of all three heavenly Persons: the perfect team.

The Word of God is much like the words uttered by the
doctor, indicating what Dwayne needed. If those words had
not been spoken, Dwayne would have died. Instead, Dwayne
"inherited" life. He lived to fight another day.

The functional words were transformed into the delivery
of real medications to Dwayne's dying body by Nurse Tina.
Without the nurse carrying out the instructions to a "T,"
Dwayne would have been as dead as a dodo.

**The Holy Spirit delivers the Word of God to humans,
resulting in life for a dead mankind.**

And the good doctor himself represents God the Father
in "Dwayne's World."

Things on earth originally worked much the same way as
things work in heaven. However, in the beginning, there was
one key difference: There were no humans in heaven. Man
was on earth.

*And God said, Let <u>us</u> make man in our own image, after
our likeness. Genesis 1:26.*

Now, here's the thing: In which of God's images were
we made? The Father's? Or the Son's? Or, possibly, the Holy
Spirit's? Which one do we look like? We'll consider a couple
of Bible passages which hopefully will give us some insight
into our resemblance to God.

Jesus explained in simple terms what the spirit was for a teacher who was having some difficulty grasping the concept. He described how a human spirit, alive to God, manifests itself.

The <u>wind</u> bloweth where it listeth, and <u>thou hearest the sound thereof, but canst not tell whence it cometh, and wither it goeth</u>; so is every one that is born of the Spirit. John 3:8.

What was Jesus saying? That a spirit cannot be quantified structurally, but you can feel its effects. A born-again spirit is *measured by what it does*, not *how it looks*.

Jesus Christ also described how God is to be worshipped by mankind.

God is a Spirit: and they that worship him <u>must</u> worship him in spirit and in truth. John 4:24.

This literally translates to: "God is measured by what he does and not how he looks. You love and honor him by carrying out his instructions." This is a pretty straightforward rendition of what initially appears to be an abstract Bible passage.

In fact, Jesus' statement reveals a hidden truth about the term "God." It is a functional or action word.

God is simultaneously a noun and a verb.

The word "God" really becomes difficult to grasp when looked at through any other lens. If treated as a pure noun, this is what God looks like....

Actually, I don't know how the Father looks. We only know that he has a face and a back, as Moses was allowed to see his back (Exodus 33:20-23). There was no mention of "side" effects.

The Holy Spirit appeared as tongues of fire on one occasion, on the Day of Pentecost (Acts 2:3-4), and in the form of a *bird,* on the day of Jesus' baptism (Luke 3:22). There still is debate about whether we had a Black Jesus or White Jesus. Some opt for the politically correct compromise: a dark-skinned, White Jesus.

A fiery bird, a back, a front, a White, Black, or *café au lait* Jew: How do any of those descriptions sound like an image of the human race? Have you looked at yourself in the mirror lately? Unless Adam was some sort of freaky, fiery, multi-colored birdman with no sides, the Bible sounds almost schizophrenic.

But if God is an "action" word and man is made in God's image, then *man* also is a functional, or action, word. Interestingly, God called both the first man and his wife *the same name* — Adam — when he made them (Genesis 5:2). Let's see if we have better luck using an action model to explain humanity.

Humans, or all "descendants of Adam," each are made up of three parts. These parts are supposed to work together perfectly, and did, under the direct instruction of God, during those early days in the Garden of Eden.

The spirit is the head. The mind or soul is the enforcer. The body is the inheritor.

Three parts in one body: The perfect team.

Do you now see how important man is in the scheme of creation? He was made as tangible, living evidence of the God Trinity: three in one. Could we look like *all three?* Yes, we can — and do. God shows his glory to all of creation.

Look at man! This is how we work!

For man indeed ought not to cover his head, forasmuch he is the <u>image</u> and <u>glory</u> of God. 1 Corinthians 11:7.

Jesus said a living spirit is *measured by what it does*, not *how it looks*. In the kingdom of God, all three parts function together, and the results of their activity are validated by visible, tangible results. Therefore, man is first and foremost a functional unit, using *all three parts* to do God's will here on earth. The better a person functions, obeying God's instructions for *all three areas* of his or her being, the more magnificent and fruitful that person's outcomes are. God's kingdom has come: in you.

Whereunto shall I liken the kingdom of God? It is like leaven, which a woman took and hid in <u>three measures</u> of meal, till the whole was leavened. Luke 13:21.

And when he was demanded of the Pharisees, when the kingdom of God should come, he answered them and said, The kingdom of God cometh not with observation: Neither shall they say, Lo here! Or, lo there! for, behold, the kingdom of God is <u>within you</u>. Luke 17:20-21.

The yeast is the Word of God. The woman is the Holy Spirit. The three measures represent the human spirit, soul, and body.

Thinking "function" opens our eyes up to the fullest expression of the kingdom of God. We start to notice the concept of three parts functioning as one, in other areas. Consider the family unit.

Father is the head. Mother is the enforcer. The children are the inheritors.

What about the corporate structure?

Shareholders are the head. The CEO is the enforcer. The employees are the inheritors.

The same rules, the same end result: the functional kingdom of God.

On numerous occasions, Jesus Christ instructed us to think functionally, not structurally, when we consider spiritual matters.

Jesus told his disciples that John the Baptist was Elijah or Elias—in *function*.

And his disciples asked him, saying, Why then say the scribes that Elias must first come? And Jesus answered and said unto them, Elias truly shall first come... But I say unto you, That Elias is come already and they knew him not, but have done unto him whatever they listed... Then the disciples understood that he spake unto them of John the Baptist. Matthew 17:10-13.

Jesus spoke of *functional* spiritual birth to the Pharisee leader Nicodemus, when he talked about being born again.

Nicodemus saith unto him, How can a man be born when he is old? can he enter the second time into his mother's womb, and be born? Jesus answered... That which is born of flesh is flesh; and that which is born of the Spirit is spirit. John 3:4-6.

Nicodemus was thinking *form*. Jesus was speaking *function*. Man is primarily a functional unit.

People, therefore, must first and foremost perform God-directed actions. This is what it means to worship God in *spirit*. We need to see ourselves first in terms of spirit or function.

What can I *do*?

This, instead of mind and body or form.

How do I look and feel?

Another way to put it is as follows: When I wake up every day, my first thought should be, "How can I use the resources I have at my disposal today to affect *everybody and everything* with which I come into contact, with God's words? How can I forward God's purposes, expressed by his words, in the world today?" Take stock of your resources, big and small, and go to work.

As you can see, I did not specify any particular resource. It could be a friendly smile: Jesus Christ to your *mind*.

A merry heart maketh a cheerful countenance... The light of the eyes rejoiceth the heart. Proverbs 15:13, 30.

Smile! Find something to smile about, even when you don't feel like it. It takes away depression and anxiety in you and in others!

It could mean imparting a godly system of doing things that you have just discovered, such as healthy eating habits: Jesus Christ to your *body*. Or it could be God showing you a value system that develops your moral conscience: Jesus Christ to your *spirit*.

Love your enemies, do good to them which hate you... For if ye love them which love you, what thank have ye? for sinners also love those that love them. Luke 6:27, 32.

Look for ways to help your enemies know God, rather than looking for ways to avenge yourself.

On a good day, it could be all of these. Function, function, *function*, until at the end of your day, you have emptied yourself into other people. You'll find that something strange and miraculous happens: You'll wake up the next morning with a whole new bag of resources and start all over again!

Somehow, the smile is still there, the kind word, and there is fulfillment. There is always somebody else with whom to share a wise word.

You'll suddenly find yourself with superhuman stamina because God's kingdom is come on earth, in you. You are doing what you were born to do.

You are resting—in motion.

For we which have believed do enter into <u>rest</u>... the works were finished from the foundation of the world. Hebrews 4:3.

LAST WORDS

Let's do an interesting exercise. Let's look at Moses seeing God's back using an action model.

And I will take away mine hand, and thou shalt see my back parts: but my face shall not be seen. Exodus 33:23.

Using God is an action word, God's face would be all the things in front of him, or all the things he will do in the future.

His back includes all the things he already has done since the beginning of time.

That's how Moses was able to write the Book of Genesis.

THE POLITICIAN

᠅

"Run the numbers, Bo."

He straightened out his shirt cuffs, the light glinting on his immaculate cufflinks, as he settled back, more comfortably, in his plush chair.

"We're up to sixty-one. We need six more, Sir." Bo cleared his throat and then launched into a crisp, professional, detailed litany on the men behind the numbers. "Senator Politski continues to hold out. We can't find any chinks. Wife has expensive tastes, but there's nothing overtly wrong with that. He can afford it."

"Everyone has a button. His boys?"

"No dirt there. Stan is the CEO of Fritsco lumber company. Good stocks. Honest worker, according to all accounts. The younger one, Ken, still is in pre-med. GPA of 3.9. He has a reputation around campus as a straight shooter. Daughter married to a banker in Tennessee. Housewife, active in the local church. No red flags."

The politician drummed his fingers thoughtfully on the smooth dark mahogany table top. "Let's leave Erasmus Politski alone for now. We'll get back to him. Dan Barker?"

"Senator Barker seems to have a gambling problem. Well hidden, of course, but there's always a paper trail. Took quite a bit of digging to find, though."

"Excellent! Rope him in gently. Make 598-EX a gamble vote for him. He has a gambler's heart; a rebel by nature. My gut tells me he needs gentle nudging; we may not need to lean on him. We can always use what we know another day."

"Yes, Sir. Senator Montgomery's daughter had an abortion in '92. Paid for by daddy."

"Good. Set up a golf date for this week. I'll tap into his pro-choice leanings. Who'd have guessed Mr. Uptight was a closet liberal?" He chuckled, permitting Bo to grin.

Methodically, efficiently, the politician and his assistant dissected the strengths and frailties of the other three candidates, reducing their lives to mincemeat, to be examined ruthlessly under their perceptive, unforgiving microscope. After a while, they returned to Erasmus Politski, the senator from Illinois.

"Check the daughter out, the one married to the banker. Look for any substance abuse vices. Could be a bored housewife. Just a hunch."

"Already checked, Sir. Squeaky clean, though she is in the peak age range for that stuff. She's thirty-two."

"Check for crystal meth; it's big in Tennessee. You don't need a dealer for that. Popular among housewives."

"I'd forgotten that, Sir." Bo, slightly annoyed with himself, straightened up from his customary slouch. "I'll get on it, right away."

He watched Bo leave and smiled to himself. Bo was a faithful lieutenant, extremely efficient and in total awe of him, he knew. However, it was good, once in a while, to pull him down a peg or two, show him who was boss. Put him in his place.

The politician leaned forward, absentmindedly doodling on a notepad, pondering the dilemma of Senator Politski.

He was a middle-aged man of slightly less than average height. His face was nondescript, deeply lined, and clean-shaven. Facial hair, he knew, gave an indication of character.

A clean-shaven face was anonymous, especially here in Washington. He had a full head of mainly dull grey hair, and favored expensive wool suits and silk ties in muted colors on his slight frame, giving him a look of quiet competence.

He had allegiance to neither Democrat nor Republican parties, though he belonged to one. He really didn't care if God existed or not, though he used Christian rhetoric to fan the flame of religious hypocrisy when he had to. He only had one goal: to change country policy—and, ultimately, world policy—to predetermined standards.

His eyes, flat and dead as a snake's when no one was around to truly see him as he was, turned introspective and reflective as he considered this bill's journey, like so many others over the years. The Toxic Waste Disposal Bill of '82 required hazardous waste to be processed in reinforced protected buildings, preventing environmental pollution. The Coalminer's Safety Bill, introduced in 1989, changed the standard specifications of mining masks and shafts.

The Religious Integration Bill of 1995 created a goal of religious uniformity from a newly crafted religious book— using excerpts from Christian, Muslim, Taoist, Wiccan, and atheist literature—adapted to the modern American society, targeted as a progressive reference book for the Judicial branch of government by 2012. A Health Insurance Autonomy Bill, which enabled individual health insurance companies to operate with total freedom regarding prices to consumers—with quarterly updates depending on expressed dividends—had floated through Congress in 2000.

All had been created and birthed in his head. They had drifted out insidiously but persistently, through the House of Representatives and the Senate, sometimes with the President's executive blessing, at other times without. That depended on the bill and, of course, the President. He'd influenced several, outlasting them all.

Then there was this bill. One more cog in the wheel; one more.

"So, Danny, here's the way the cards fall." The politician leaned forward, engaging Senator Dan Barker with a look of earnest transparency. "If it works, *if* the grafted embryonic tissue actually starves out the cancerous tissue selectively, we have a universal cure for cancer on our hands. Given what we know now, this is more than feasible; it's a reality.

"The squeamishness regarding the ethical issues of using embryonic stem cells will be tempered by the sheer number of cancer cases. It's a whole different ball game from spinal cord injuries and Parkinson's disease, which—let's face it— are neither as frequent nor scary.

"But then again, when we back this," he held Senator Barker's gaze, "the American people are unpredictable. You know how this issue divides along party lines. It's a huge gamble." He quickly shifted his gaze to one of contemplative intensity. "But think of the dividends. As you'll be backing this from the beginning, it will become your brainchild, your defining moment." He casually went in for the kill, almost as an afterthought: "People like that kind of pioneering spirit in their legislators. Or even presidents, for that matter. If you know what I mean."

Senator Barker sniffed. "Well, you and I know one thing for sure: this President won't go for it. It's the wrong kind of political risk for him." He took another drink of strong, dark coffee. "Something tells me you weren't talking about our current Commander-in-Chief, though."

The politician smiled, knowing in that moment he had him. "No, I was not."

Eight days later, the hubbub ebbed and flowed as the unseasonably warm October evening was complemented by the animated crowd circulating between the huge ballroom and the patio deck. The pre-dinner social mingling, prior to the fundraiser, was at its max. The politician carefully meandered his way through the well turned-out bodies, creating an indirect, seemingly casual journey to his main target for the evening: Senator Politski.

He still hadn't cracked the Politski puzzle. The daughter angle had not panned out. He'd already thoroughly screened the other thirty-something senators, and he had eventually eliminated each one. Not because he couldn't bend one of them to his will, but because he would overtly expose himself and his motives by doing so. He sighed impatiently. The Senate, with its insincere ideological pomposity, was proving to be a pain in the backside. The Reps, for which he already had a comfortable, three-hundred-plus group of backers, were much easier to deal with: much more materialistic.

"Ras Politski! Good to see you again! What a nice evening."

He adjusted his glasses—clear lens glasses worn for effect, although he had perfect vision. "A perfect evening to part rich men from their money."

Senator Erasmus Politski laughed, throwing back his leonine head. "Not the perfect evening for me, though. I have to start laxative colon preps tonight after this sumptuous dinner. Colonoscopy tomorrow afternoon. I hate drinking that stuff, but I guess a check once a decade isn't so bad. When's yours coming up? You're what, now? Sixty? Sixty-one?"

"Nah. Just fifty-nine years young."

The politician deftly kept the banter going, but he was hard put to keep the triumphant gleam out of his eye. He had found Politski's chink.

"Run the numbers."

"Three hundred and two reps, sixty-eight senators. Senators Barker, Montgomery, and...," Bo paused, "Politski, are all a go. And a surprise freebee, Senator Donahue."

"Excellent! Are you sure? Let's go over them again."

The two of them painstakingly went over the three hundred and seventy names. Three hundred and seventy congressmen and women, who would vote in the "Stem Cancer" Bill as law. No matter what the Chief Executive of the nation, the President of the United States of America, thought. The politician had his two-thirds majority.

Several hours later, Bo looked at his boss and asked the question that had been on his mind all week long: "Sir, if you don't mind my asking, how did you turn Senator Politski?"

The politician stretched, regarding his understudy. "By working deep in the trenches." He savored the look of confusion on Bo's face. "I'll give you a clue: It lies with his son, Ken, the pre-med one. Dad listened to his son."

There still was no comprehension from Bo. The politician finally relented. "He talked Politski into getting a colonoscopy."

"Politski may be clean, but what about his doctor? Let's just say that for now, the honorable Senator Politski believes he has stage three colon carcinoma. It sure changes your perspective on cancer, when you have it. Or think you do. The rest was easy, borrowed from Socrates." He loved to use aspects of Socratic philosophy, a series of casually placed simple questions, each of which had an obviously logical "Yes" answer. They all were links in a chain to the big conclusion, which he had made his targets think they had arrived at by themselves.

They would now take his conclusion and proclaim it as their own, garnering political attention and accolades. Vanity and greed: This was exactly what he wanted. Let them be his face. But every once in a while, he had to sink to less savory methods of persuasion. His methods were honed and perfected in the deep, dark sinkhole of his youth, the early days, the days of fries and ketchup.

Bo shook his head in awe and admiration. "I don't know how you do it. I really don't."

"No, you don't." The politician tapped him on the shoulder, his mind already on his next project. This would be the last cog in the wheel, before it really began: the Satellite Surveillance Bill. Simple formulas for far-reaching solutions. He worked in thirds.

All I need is one third. Then I'll get the second third. Then, I've won.

"Brilliant work; go catch yourself some shut-eye. See you in the morning."

The politician dispassionately put on his overcoat. "It's a good thing, for his own sake, that he changed his mind."

And with that, the politician, the most dangerous man in Washington, turned out the light and left the room.

THE KINGDOM OF SATAN AND THE CONCEPT OF THIRDS
PART I: THE METHOD

※

A ll spirits give instructions.
Being human means having a body, soul, and spirit.
The human spirit receives instructions from other spirits.
Let's learn a few more nuggets about the human spirit.
How does it give instructions?

By examining all the mind's thoughts, it gives instructions based on what it sees.

The spirit of man is the candle of the LORD, searching all the inward parts of the belly. Proverbs 20:27.

Conscience is, therefore, housed in the human spirit. But how does conscience get there? Or, more broadly, how does the human spirit *receive* instructions? The human spirit either *receives messages* or *becomes occupied*.

The receipt of messages is an external method of control. Received messages are either used or discarded by the recipient. In other words, the *recipient's* reputation is at stake, regardless of whether he or she decides to use the message.

As for becoming occupied, this is an internal method of control. The sender moves into—and sends instructions directly out from—the human spirit. Choice is surrendered to the sender. Therefore, the *sender's* reputation is at stake, depending on the observed outcome.

If external control is using a fitness book to exercise, internal control is hiring its writer as your live-in, personal trainer.

Good! Now that we've tucked away those useful knowledge nuggets, we can talk shop: about war.

An old Chinese general once said, "When one has a thorough knowledge of both the enemy and oneself, victory is assured."

He wrote the timeless masterpiece on wartime combat maneuvers, used by multiple generations of military strategists, over hundreds of years. His name is Sun Tzu, and his book is *The Art of War: A Treatise on Chinese Military Science*. It's heavy reading—which is why I haven't read it. But the quote is smart and insightful.

Some of you may be asking, "What do Sun Tzu and his treatise have to do with my life?" Well, the answer is that, whether or not we are aware of it, we are at war.

For we wrestle not against flesh and blood, but against principalities, against powers, against the rulers of the darkness of this world, against spiritual wickedness in high places. Ephesians 6:12.

For the weapons of our warfare are not carnal, but mighty through God to the pulling down of strong holds. 2 Corinthians 10:4.

Wrestling evil spirits, possessing warfare weapons: If that's not war, then what is? It is not a war of our own choosing, but it is a war, nonetheless.

Satan is the villain of this piece. He is real; he heads an army of fallen angels or demons and has specific modes of operation in this peculiar war. It is, therefore, to our advantage to possess a better understanding of who our enemy is and how he works.

We need to know whom we are fighting.

How does Satan attack man? How does it all work? Well, Satan's activities can be broadly divided into two groups: the way he stays effective for himself, and the way he destroys people.

Satan stays effective for himself by putting his function before his form.

Satan, when he was Lucifer, made a mistake within the kingdom of heaven. He thought his perfect looks and wisdom should earn him a different job. He put his form before his function, with devastating consequences. He lost his place in God's kingdom.

Satan is smart. He also is extremely old; he has had plenty of time to mull over his mistakes. He learned from failure, and he now puts his function before his form. Ironically, however, this is what makes him so effective.

He actually is piggybacking off the laws of the kingdom of God. It also is easy because his form has lost its luster, as he is no longer alive to God. Think of a beautiful but dead body—that's how he looks these days. There's really not much to show off any more. Isaiah made an astute observation.

They that see thee shall narrowly look upon thee, and consider thee, saying, Is this the man that made the earth to tremble, that did shake kingdoms; That made the world as a wilderness. Isaiah 14:16-17.

Ouch! To say that Satan was not pleased by that particular piece of revealing Scripture is an understatement. He doesn't like descriptions of himself. That makes him too noticeable. Much like the politician, he blends in, working deep in the trenches. He is an unseen puppeteer, changing nations.

Satan grabs people one third at a time.

People are not a homogenous group. There are all kinds of people: Christians, "Christianoids"—the "almost Christians" who *say* they believe Jesus Christ is God's Son but don't *act* like it—Muslims, Buddhists, atheists, etc. However, for being such a mixed bag, people tend to follow certain patterns of behavior which are actually quite predictable.

Some are strictly logical thinkers who act based on facts alone. Others act on impulse, based on how they feel. Then there are the "faith walkers," people who grab a vision and run with it, usually with miraculous results. The Christianoid is a professional skeptic who does not act on *anything at all* until perfect facts and feelings align—a state of affairs as rare as Haley's Comet!

But let's get back to Satan's strategy for people. What does Satan do to people? Surprisingly, he uses the same general strategy for every single person; Jew, Gentile, Christian or politician, you're all the same to him. *You're standing in his way.*

The kingdom of God and the concept of threes purport that in God's kingdom, three parts function together as one.

What God has joined together, let no man put asunder.

The kingdom of Satan works based on a concept of *thirds*. Satan splits the one unit into thirds. He then grabs a third, making it function independently of the other two. The captured third is then used to influence and capture a second third.

He attacks the fleshly body, the easiest to get, in terms of physical illness or fleshly needs.

He attacks the mind—usually by affecting the "feeling" portion or mood—with anxiety, depression, or fear, or the "logical" portion, which relies too much on facts or strict scientific thought.

He attacks the spirit, the hardest third, to turn through external control—the most common form of Satanic influence—or internal control. The latter may involve involuntary indwelling, in which Satanic spirits or demons mingle with an individual's spirit, or voluntary indwelling through devil worship like Satanism or witchcraft.

Satan puts asunder, what God has put together.

It's as easy as pie, and he keeps recycling the same method because it *works*. As we will see below, Satan's attack *always* involves these areas, though he applies different starting points to different people.

An attack usually starts on either the mind or the fleshly body. Satan will not go for the spirit—especially of a Christian—unless he is desperate; it is the hardest third to turn.

An example of this would be falling sick physically. You start to question why this has happened to you. You ponder these events deeply, feeling more and more anxious about returning to work, earning a living, etc. This leads to anxiety, depression, or other thoughts. You start to hate your own body. At that point, your mind—the second third—has been captured.

The other scenario is that you are afflicted with an affective mood disorder, like depression. You stop exercising, even getting out of bed. Your muscles shrink and your teeth rot because you no longer care to brush them; you choose to lie in bed all day instead. This is based, of course, on how you *feel*. Things go from bad to worse with you wasting away your days, staring at a wall, and hating yourself. You attempt suicide to end it all.

The fundamental error is using the physical or mental ailment as a *beginning* point for further action. It is a deception, as your *spirit*—not your mind or body—is supposed to initiate events. Your spirit's instructions are then supposed to be validated in your body and mental state. Anything less, and a third of you has broken rank and gone rogue. In Jesus' words, a house divided against itself cannot stand.

Every kingdom divided against itself is brought to desolation; and every city or house divided against itself shall not stand. Matthew 12:25.

Senator Dan Barker illustrates the manipulation of the "feeling" mind. He was manipulated, using his rebellious "heart," his "I go against the grain," feelings. His need to gamble reveals him as an impulsive dreamer.

Senator Montgomery was easy prey, once the politician learned of the abortion. He represents the purely logical or factual thinker, the stomping ground of scientific purists. The senator would bury his conscience and sacrifice an embryo for what he logically imagined to be the greater good.

And then there is the fascinating case of the honorable senator from Illinois, Erasmus Politski. He changed his mind, when he imagined things had gotten personal, and his colon was under attack. Never mind that it was a slickly enacted deception. That didn't matter.

For as he thinketh in his heart, so is he. Proverbs 23:7.

When Satan uses the mind or flesh as his starting point, he applies a foolproof way to make people lose their effectiveness. He has first-hand knowledge of how devastatingly effective this strategy is.

He deceives humans into placing form before function.

It was his ancient mistake, after all.

Now, how about attacking the spirit?

External control affects all categories of people. Such individuals unknowingly cooperate with Satan's purposes in the world. They usually will expound theories that, when examined closely, are Satanic. An example is the concept of "good debt" creating a healthy economy.

Involuntary indwelling is demon possession. A complicated topic, it is a much less common form of Satanic control. Satan's helper angels actually make a home in an individual, giving the person formidable angelic power and strength, with diabolical intent.

Voluntary indwelling—or devil worship—encompasses Satanism and witchcraft. This is the most damaging method of spiritual control. The devil worshipper's spirit is given a corrupt set of values, and the normal conscience is lost. Such people put spirit before mind and body, as was originally intended, but tweak God's methods for devilish purposes. Devil worshippers, therefore, tend to be very successful at the dark stuff they do. This is the pathology of psychopathic killers, and is epitomized in the "behind the scenes," coldly efficient and yet, awestruck Bo.

If therefore the light that is in thee be darkness, how great is that darkness! Matthew 6:23.

Now, here is a sobering truth: Satan needs only two thirds to neutralize an individual.

If he gets two thirds of you, he's won.

How can that be? *Because the spirit is useless if it fails to illuminate the mind and body.*

If the spirit is darkness, it cannot see the dark areas of the mind that need changing. And if your spirit is bright but both mind and body are consistently dancing to a different tune, it might as well be dark. The spirit's functional currency is faith, but what use is spiritual faith, when it has nothing to work on? Or, put another way, what use is your spiritual money, if there is nothing to buy?

Now faith is the substance of things hoped for, the evidence of things not seen. Hebrews 11:1.

But wilt thou know, O vain man, that faith without works is dead? James 2:20.

The spirit can have as much functional promise or "faith" as it wants, but without a template (mind or body) to work on, it is ineffective. Hope is lost, faith disappears, and the spirit is broken.

But by sorrow of the heart the spirit is broken. Proverbs 15:13.

Satan has won.

Or has he? Relax, all hope is not lost. It's time for another story.

THE VETERAN

🙢

It had been a long day. An exciting day, but a long one. The conference had started in earnest at 10 a.m. As usual, he had managed to arrive twenty minutes late. Oh, all the usual excuses applied: traffic, finding the conference location, and all that stuff. But the end result was the same.

Slightly sweaty after a vigorous half-mile walk from the parking garage to the Tabernacle in downtown Atlanta, he'd joined the group of vital men and women intent on making a positive difference in the world.

Close to twelve hours later, he was retracing his steps to the same parking garage, wearily examining his feelings as he made the harder, less vigorous half-mile walk back to his car. He was tired, elated, fulfilled—and yes, troubled—by some of the things he had learned.

As he crossed a side street, he vaguely noticed out of the corner of his eye a disheveled-looking man, probably in his early forties, walking toward him.

His first impulse was to ignore the man. From previous experience, he knew that this had a distinct possibility of not ending well. If worse came to worst, he felt he probably could take care of himself, but he was just too tired to deal with a verbal or physical scuffle right now. Besides, it would be a shame to ruin a nice coat.

But the hobo was determined. He lengthened his stride on a collision course with the well-dressed man and piped up, "Evenin,' Sir. How ya doin'? Could you help out a brother?"

So, he stopped and regarded the vagrant, silhouetted against the backdrop of a downtown that always looked sophisticated and glitzy in the day but somewhat more stark at night. A steady gaze returned his own, a gaze tinged with desperation. What he saw in those eyes was expected and unexpected.

A man; a man no different from him, really. They even were of similar height, though he had to admit, he had a little more padding than his object of study. Did his choices lead to his circumstances, or his circumstances to his choices? Did it really matter?

"Good evening. What do you need?"

"I'm hungry, man; a dollar seventy-five will help me get a meal."

He sighed inwardly. The easy solution was to give the man his wish. But they both knew there was not a hope in hell that he could get anything other than a light snack, for that kind of money. Or something that had nothing to do with food.

"I'll do better than that. Come, let's get you a meal."

"You don't have to go out of your way, Sir."

"Ah, don't worry about it. I passed an eating place a little ways back."

So, the man in the nice coat and the hobo strolled back toward an eatery.

"What's your name, man?"

"Don't worry about it."

"Where you from? You don't act like someone from around here; I'll tell you that. I used to be in the Navy, you know. Traveled all over the world: Germany, Paris, Africa."

He let the man who had fallen on unfortunate times speak. He silently wondered why Africa was always referred to as if it was one big country. Loud rap music blasted out of the eatery, interjected with "shout-outs" from an onsite deejay. The vagrant ate to his heart's content.

"God bless you, man! *What is* your name?"

"I said don't worry about it. You have a good night."

He resumed his half-mile trek with more buoyancy. I guess he was lighter; he had just shed some dollars. He thought about the veteran, and the man's need to name and be named. He wanted to say, "You already know my name: It is man; so is yours."

I still would have helped you, even if you had not been a veteran.

THE KINGDOM OF SATAN AND THE CONCEPT OF THIRDS
PART II: THE ANTIDOTE

※

S o, how do we fight Satan?
The solution to Satan's method is quite simply: love. It's Satan's antidote.

Make love *and* war.

Believe it or not, love is the foundation stone to beating Satan in all wars. Satan has no love in him; only hate. Love is toxic to him so *make love and war!* God's way is love and this deactivates Satan, who is ruled by hate and revenge.

He that loveth not is not of God, For God is love. 1 John 4:8.

Jesus Christ's summary of all God's instructions was to love God and love all people, including oneself.

Jesus said unto him, Thou shalt love the Lord thy God with all thy heart, and with all thy soul, and with all thy mind. This is the first and great commandment. And the second is like unto it, Thou shalt love thy neighbour as thyself. On these two commandments hang all the law and the prophets. Matthew 22:37-40.

Love is an action, more than a feeling. If you love someone, you want to know more about them and help them. How do we do this practically?

Learn to notice people. Pick someone outside of your usual circle of friends and family each day. Deliberately observe them for a few moments, long enough to learn something about them. Before you go to bed, try to recall the individual and what you observed. You can write down your observation, if you need an aid to remember; this is not a memory competition, but love training. *You can't love what you don't notice.*

Then shall they also answer him, saying, Lord, <u>when saw we thee</u> an hungred, or athirst, or a stranger, or naked, or sick, or in prison, and did not minister unto thee? Matthew 25:44.

Look for the good in people. Now you're in the habit of noticing people other than your mother. While observing your random pick, commit to memory one thing about that person that you like: anything at all. Recall it later. I know this is hard, but you are in training; keep trying, and you will see it. Contrary to popularly held opinion, *good still exists, every place on earth.*

Holy, holy, holy, is the Lord of hosts: <u>the whole earth</u> is full of his glory. Isaiah 6:3.

Look for the needs of people. OK, observation guru; it's time to step it up a notch. Look for something you don't like in your person of interest. In other words, something you would rather not see in them. *You've identified that person's need, or their sickness.* My sickness is something existing in me that shouldn't be there.

And Jesus answering said unto them, They that are whole need not a physician; but they that are sick. Luke 5:31.

That's all you need to learn for now. You have just learned Love 101.

Don't worry; your love actions will come, because you automatically start taking stock of what you have, and if you can fulfill a need. It could be as simple as a focused smile or compliment to wipe away a frown on a potentially bad day.

Do you know if your smile was the difference between life and death that day? If it prevented someone from going "postal" or committing suicide? Or if the giving of a meal prevented someone from taking one by force, using techniques he learned in the military? How well have we really loved people? The answers to some commonly held practices may surprise you.

Most movies, including *The Chronicles of Narnia*, have the famous movie stars smoking cigarettes, cigars, or pipes, and looking elegant doing it. *Didn't I read somewhere that four hundred and forty thousand Americans die from smoking each year?*

What about the use of the word "alien"—legal or not? *Surely illegal residents, even strangers, would be a friendlier term.*

Then there are the computer games whose whole aim and purpose is to kill or maim imaginary computer characters. *So, how does killing an imaginary computer man help me love my neighbor?*

What about promising to set captives free, like a big brother would, but not learning the name of the people, region, or country you are supposedly saving? A foreign last name becomes "Mr. Whatever-his-name-is;" mission trips are to that big "country" of Africa; the nation Myanmar still gets called by the oppressive colonial name of Burma, and Iraq is consistently mispronounced *Eye*-raq. *What kind of a big brother are you? You're here to set me "free," but you aren't interested enough in me to learn my name?*

These examples are by no means harmless. The above passage says that if we do not love others, we are not of God. We are *all* created in God's image! James wrote about the words we utter, the actions we condone, and how damaging they can be.

Therewith bless we God, even the Father; and therewith curse we men, which are made after the similitude of God. James 3:9.

Satan looks for ways to disobey the rules of God's kingdom and cause internal strife or hate among mankind. It was his technique in heaven among the angels. After Satan and his followers had been defeated and thrown out of heaven, the heavenly angels heaved a huge sigh of relief. Satan had been getting on their nerves. This information shared with you today is empowerment, if used. It's a labor of love.

And they overcame him by the blood of the Lamb, and by the word of their testimony. Revelation 12:11.

We must learn to recognize Satan's patterns.

How do you recognize a Satan-driven spirit? By his functional intent; after all, a spirit is best defined by what it achieves.

First, simplify; get to the bottom line. Get into the habit of asking: "So, what are the underlying take-home messages of this movie, recommendation, or position statement? Do they line up with the word of God?" If not, you are witnessing the handiwork of a spirit controlled by Satan, usually from several notches higher up the ladder, rather than the puppet speaker, or actor.

Forget how or by whom the statement is made. This is because it makes you reliant on form—the messenger and his historical track record, or lack of it—rather than function, or the actual message itself. If a decent spokesperson goes off track, so do you. Satan loves charisma to do his work.

Do not be susceptible to wolves in sheep's clothing. The politician from the previous story had masterminded bills on both the left and the right of political debates, making friends on both sides in the process. But as we can see, his ultimate agenda was neither left, nor right. Neither side could see this; all they saw was a reliable, non-threatening individual, a quiet man who gave wise counsel.

Test everything in God's word—everything! See if a behavior or statement lines up, without apologies, with God's words on the subject. Good actions always come from God no matter who does them, and should be championed.

Let's look at a practical example. A Nigerian professor a few years ago invented a refrigeration system that does not require electricity, the "pot-in-pot refrigerator." It uses two earthenware pots, one inside the other with wet sand between them. The water in the wet sand evaporates using the heat from the inner pot, reducing the temperature of the inner pot by up to twenty five degrees Fahrenheit.

It helps provide food in arid areas of drought, keeping spinach and other items fresh for weeks rather than days, saving hundreds of lives in affected areas of the world, lives that don't have access to electricity. *But he is Mohammed Bah Abba, a Muslim.*

I have never seen a single TV ad from missionary Christians—you know, the "dollar-a-day" ads that provide clean drinking water to poor people in the places we believe God forgot—specifically acknowledge this wonderful technology, widen its distribution, and save lives. Why? Because it didn't come from a professed Christian. We are too caught up with the messenger, and not enough with the message.

May I remind you that God called the famous King Nebuchadnezzar of Babylon, an unholy king by all accounts, his *servant*, and used the king to do his work in the earth? Or that an Egyptian pharaoh was sent by God on a specific mission, to the chagrin of Josiah, a holy Israelite king, the story recounted in 2 Chronicles 35? That the infamous Pontius Pilate's wife begged her then-governor husband to not condemn Jesus to death, because *God* showed her Jesus was innocent, in a dream? Or that a *donkey*—no less—was used to minister to a crazy, stubborn prophet called Balaam?

But the lesson of Balaam is lost if we never work with a God-given innovation to save lives. If God can use donkeys to minister to a man of God, do we really think it is such a stretch that he could use other humans like ourselves to reveal the principles of his kingdom?

Hold onto your thirds.

Satan is useless unless he has a two-third majority; he can do nothing with one third. One third would appear to be Satan's initial investment. He then recruits you and I to do the rest.

There are examples of him working in thirds in Scripture. He got one third of the angels of heaven before he started fighting against God in the Book of Revelation.

Behold a great red dragon... And his tail drew the third part of the stars of heaven...And there was war in heaven:

Michael and his angels fought against the dragon; and the dragon fought and his angels. Revelation 12:3-4, 7.

He desperately tried to get two thirds of the Holy Trinity, a third at a time, when he tempted Jesus Christ. Why didn't Satan tempt Jesus before Jesus' baptism? Because Satan had to wait until the Holy Spirit had descended on Jesus like a dove. Prior to this, only one third of the Holy Trinity was officially available, which is of no use to Satan; now he had a shot at *two*. He was trying for the package deal: "Buy one, get one free."

And Jesus being full of the <u>Holy Ghost</u> returned from Jordan, and was led by the Spirit into the wilderness, Being forty days tempted of the devil. Luke 4:1-2.

Whatever mysteries of the beast of the apocalypse, one thing we do know: He has a human number, six hundred and sixty six. Someone pointed out to me, one day when I was talking about threes and thirds, that six hundred and sixty six is two thirds of a thousand. Hmm. Interesting, to say the least.

If Satan comes for your body with physical illness or fleshly impulse look for attitudes that are known to be healthy for the other two thirds: your mind and spirit.

Smile often, both inside and out. Humor is an established method of achieving this.

Meet up with encouraging, positive people. Feed off their energy.

Identify people who are disadvantaged and sick. Use yourself as a functional resource for them.

Build up your spirit. This can be done by reading the Holy Bible or a good Bible promise book.

If he comes for your mind, saturate your *spirit* in Scripture as a survival strategy, and carry out all the healthy God commands for your *body*. These include: appropriate dietary endeavor and exercise; staying away from cigarette smoke including secondhand smoke, etc.; and singing praises to God *during the Satanic attack*. Especially when you don't feel like it; it is an offensive weapon, a strategy that always works when you are attacked by Satan.

These deliberate actions will keep your two thirds in good shape. Satan can't afford to wait for you; he has too much devil work to do. He'll drop your missing third, and skulk off into the night.

Don't be a Christianoid.

For the Christianoid, both young and old, inactivity is Satan's strongest weapon. These professional fault-finders sit waiting for people to put on a show for them. They critique, and wait, and do *nothing*. And drive everybody else nuts. If it were possible, they'd drive God nuts. Jesus referred to this group directly.

Well hath Esaias prophesied of you hypocrites, as it is written, This people honoureth me with their lips, but their heart is far from me. Mark 7:6.

Whereunto then shall I liken the men of this generation? ... They are like unto children sitting in the market-place, and calling one to another, and saying, We have piped unto you and ye have not danced. Luke 7:31-32.

So then because thou art lukewarm, and neither cold nor hot, I will spue thee out of my mouth. Revelation 3:16.

Unfortunately, if you are a full-time Christianoid, you are a non-Christian, even if you've filled church pews since you were a day old. Being a Christianoid goes against the way we were created. It totally contradicts every principle of God's kingdom. But God's kingdom here on earth will continue, with or without you. After all, God has said he will raise up stones to worship him, if need be.

The only opportunity to bring man to an understanding of God and change his eternal destination is during the time we have been given, when we are physically alive. What kind of gospel of life are we preaching about, when our target audience is diminishing rapidly from physical death? We might as well go preach to headstones in a cemetery, if we think their deaths every year, both physical and spiritual, are not our concern.

If Jesus instructed us to go and make disciples of Jesus Christ in deed, thought, and action, can you remember the last time you actually led a soul to repentance? Not to a church building, or to a church small group, but to the actual rebirth of that human spirit, with the emergence of a sincere follower of the truth, Jesus Christ?

If global warming is causing drought and millions of deaths yearly, it is of Satan. Christians need not ignore the information—even if it seems to be talked about by an unlikely source of information to Christians.

If diabetes mellitus correlates with up to ninety percent of cases with obesity—if we have over seventy thousand directly attributable yearly deaths in the U.S. from this disease as well as untold suffering from it, and if it is related to our traditional church barbecue cuisine—then our "holy" church dietary habits are *Satanic*. Why are we waiting to *feel* like changing those eating habits?

If more than ten percent of all humanity alive today will die from illness related to cigarette smoking—six hundred and fifty million—then, as Christians, we have to take it personally and do *something*. We cannot fold our hands and say, "Well, thank God I don't smoke!"

God has waited—and has now been compelled to use unlikely sources—to get his will done on a continuum which could, embarrassingly for mankind, end up with God using rocks to do his will, if we are not careful. Since God's chosen people won't prophecy on issues of daily living, God has raised up other people as prophets. But we don't believe them. We are waiting for God to perform.

If we stubbornly wait for facts and feelings to function, Satan has done what he set out to do: neutralize and destroy.

Now we know whom we are fighting.

The thief cometh not, but for to steal, and to kill, and to destroy. John 10:10.

LAST WORDS

Here's something interesting! Look at the very first recorded temptation in the Holy Bible and the subsequent fall of man. Let's look closely at the anatomy of a fall.

And the serpent said unto the woman, Ye shall not surely die... And when the woman saw that the tree was good for food, and that it was pleasant to the eyes, and a tree to be desired to make one wise, she took of the fruit thereof and did eat. Genesis 3:4, 6.

The serpent is the spirit of Satan (in function).
The fruit was good for food, which addresses the fleshly body (form).
It was pleasant to the eye, which addresses "feeling" thought or the heart (form).
The desire for wisdom addresses logical thought or the mind (form).

The woman *ate*; she placed form before function. Satan got his two thirds. The result was spiritual death. Her spirit could not "veto" a two-thirds majority.

By stark contrast, let's look at the temptation of Jesus Christ, after a forty-day fast, exposure to the elements, and wild beasts. Look at the antidote, his successful battle with Satan.

And when the tempter came to him, he said, If thou be the Son of God, command that these stones be made bread. But he answered and said, It is written... then the devil taketh him up into the holy city... If thou be the Son of God, cast thyself down... Jesus said unto him, It is written... the devil taketh him up into an exceeding high mountain... And saith unto him, All these things will I give thee, if thou wilt fall down and worship me. Then saith Jesus unto him, Get thee hence, Satan: for it is written... Then the devil leaveth him. Matthew 4:3-11.

The tempter was the spirit of Satan (in function).
Turning stones to bread addresses the fleshly body (form).
The idea of casting thyself down with no injury addresses the mind's ego or pride (form).
To fall down and worship Satan addresses the spirit (function).

Jesus' response of: "It is written..." is the same for all three temptations, demonstrating function over form.
The result was that Satan couldn't get a third. He was done, so off he went.
There was nothing left to tempt.

THE KING OF THE HILL

T he two princes squared off, looking intently at each other, damage on their minds as they prepared for battle. Two formidable men, on opposite sides, each dedicated, with deadly intent to winning. It was a fight for survival and justification in their minds, a cause worth fighting for; it meant everything.

Victor glanced up to the overcast sky, gauging the weather. It was a good day to fight. It wasn't one of the blistering, energy-sapping days that had been more the norm of late. He flexed and extended his fingers, limbering up. It was a good day to win.

Godwin was going through preparations of his own, going through a mental check list of where all his body parts were in space. His fighting style revolved around suppleness and stealth, unlike Victor's, which hinged on power and speed. He also looked to the skies for a moment. It looked as if it might rain, an edge for him, he thought. It was a good day to fight; a good day to die.

They had agreed not to start fighting until both were absolutely ready. There were no witnesses, except the gentle kiss of a slight breeze, rustling dead brown leaves on desiccated-looking trees.

Neither man had a family. Neither had any troops left, though they were said to each have commanded hundreds of thousands of men, in a sophisticated masterpiece of modern war: a war that had involved remote destruction of targets, stealth missions, economic blockade and the like, with privileged people becoming even more obscenely rich from wartime contracts.

It was all good for big business until one side, to prove superior strength, decided to detonate a nuclear weapon, and promptly torched the atmosphere. Things clipped along a whole lot faster after that. Unfortunately, money couldn't buy a new sky.

So finally, after death and more death, there were two men left standing. The two leaders who had headed each superpower, each born to win. Two commanders who had sent troops to fight in a fierce battle to validate a way of life until there were no more troops to send. Two men who had watched their families diminish steadily, gradually becoming casualties of the Great War, until there was nothing left.

So, it all came down to this: one last fight.

The two kings squared off. Victor looked intently at his opponent, ready to go. The first few drops of yellow rain fell. Godwin nodded slightly. It was time.

Hours—or minutes—later, it was over with one fatal blow. There was nothing but silence, broken only by the heavy breathing of the victor, triumphant after a hard-won fight, and the relentless patter of the oily-looking rain.

He raised up his head, the rain slicking down his hair, his fists raised to heaven. "I've won! Thank God! What a fight!" He looked for someone to celebrate with, gleeful in victory.

But only silence greeted him. He somewhat confusedly finally looked around, seeing his world for the first time in years.

His gaze took in barren earth, sparsely dotted with shriveled trees. Dirty brown leaves, mostly on the ground, a few still clinging desperately to knobby branches. No birds chirping. No distant dogs barking. He couldn't even spot any earthworms in the muddy earth.

"It was the right thing to do. To demonstrate that our way—my way—was right! I had to win this for all... for all... austerity!" But with a sinking feeling, his heart told him a different story.

You idio...I mean naughty fellow, there is no austerity! Everything you were fighting for is gone. Even the sun refused to witness this fight.

And so he sat down on a tree stump, majestic in victory and yet tragic in defeat, his skin slick with rain and maybe a tear or two; who could tell? Finally, he was undeniably what he had always wanted to be. What he believed he was born to be. The king of the hill.

Mrs. Brothers came out on the back porch.

"Victor! Godwin! It's time to eat! Where *are* you boys?"

"Over here, Mom!" Godwin popped up from his sprawled "dead" position. He quickly dusted the brown leaves off his clothes, leaving several brown dirt splotches.

He grinned over at Victor, whose hair was slightly misted over by the gentle September drizzle.

"Next time, you play dead! It's boring lying in the grass, doing nothing."

"All right, all right! Stop fussing already!" And then, toward the back porch: "Coming!"

The "Great War" was officially over. The Brothers boys trotted indoors.

COMPETITION

It is impossible to cover all aspects of how Satan attacks mankind in one small book. In the two previous chapters, we tried to cover the main modes of his attack, in what, I hope, was a simple, easy-to-understand format.

However, such a discussion is incomplete if it does not address the phenomenon of competition, and what a pivotal role this seemingly harmless daily endeavor plays in the kingdoms of God and Satan.

As always, the answers are found at the very beginning of things.

In the beginning God created the heaven and the earth. Genesis 1:1.

Now, God is the creator of all things.

Did creating make God any better, or more holy than he already was?

The answer is no. However, God started making a bunch of things, stopping periodically to evaluate the quality of his creation and pronouncing it "good," until all the universe was created.

I'd like to put words to the thoughts of God at the beginning of creation—though these can only in a limited way express the magnitude of the thought process and the ensuing events.

"I am everything perfect, and good and wonderful, in all possible permutations and expressions of these words. I am going to make things, tangible things, things that will represent just how glorious I am. Each time I make a new creature or thing, it represents another aspect of my vision of perfection. But I've got more in me, more where that came from. So, I'll make some more! It all looks great! It still isn't complete, though. I've got one last thing to create: a chip off the old block. He will be like me."

This whole process of creation, if looked at critically, was a process of *competition*.

The word "compete" takes its origins from two Latin words: *com* which means together, and *petere* which means to seek or strive.

God, in three Persons, strove together consciously and purposefully for an objective or prize, which was the creation of the whole universe.

God was competing with himself.

Man is a functional representation of the Godhead and is imbued with the same competitive spirit that is seen in his maker, God himself.

I was made to compete with myself.

As we remember from earlier discussion, God was literally making it known to all creation that man was the glory of God, the culmination of his creation and his ambassador on earth. This is just one aspect of the creation process, a process so intricate that it made King David exclaim,

I will praise thee; for I am fearfully and wonderfully made. Psalm 139:14.

The representation of God in man was so complete, so viscerally representative of the Godhead, that after the first man and woman were made, inspected, and pronounced "very good," God stopped creating, and has not crafted another creature since then.

It is, therefore, not at all surprising that we are all born with the natural, instinctual drive to compete. This shows up very early in our development, and is seen and most fully understood in a newborn baby.

They strive and struggle, for that wonderful first breath of air. Quickly mastering the art of breathing, they determinedly honk their horns in search of fuel. They practice using their muscles, aimlessly at first. At three weeks, a baby has learned to use those muscles more purposefully. It can—temporarily at least—hold up its head.

They melt our hearts with a smile at six weeks. A three-month-old sits, without collapsing to one side, in a tangled heap. Six months, and they're off to the races, crawling everywhere! Within a year, a baby is eating real pureed food; standing and in most cases "cruising;" has learned to manipulate you with a smile, cry, or sometimes an innocently vacant look; and has developed a taste for your car keys.

The little tot will learn more in the first year, than he or she will learn in any other year of earthly life. Striving to attain every new skill set, one more step toward the "prize:" becoming a productive biped, a suave Cro-magnon. The ultimate *Homo sapiens sapiens*.

This is the blueprint, laid down by God, on how we are to compete. It is progressive, warms our hearts to see, and hurts no one.

Educated psychologists and erudite pediatricians have opted to give this kind of competition another name, one that has filtered through to regular society; it has been renamed "developmental milestones." That sounds much more civilized but, unfortunately, is another of Satan's deceptive tricks.

Competition describes *function*. Developmental milestones describe *form*.

The phraseology "developmental milestone" evokes a mental image of how the baby *looks*, peering through a snapshot in time. Competition describes what the infant *does* over a period of time. Once again, a subtle change in wording alters the originally intended emphasis, hiding an important lesson. Woe betide that we have a healthy template to work from!

This now sets the stage for the next degree of deception. Competition gets redefined.

Competition becomes about striving *against* one another for a prize.

This is the single most lethal poison of humanity, because it introduces the "I am better than you" syndrome. Why is this so dangerous?

It creates laziness. Your best is now defined by your fellow competitor's best. Your ceiling becomes your opponent's highest achievement, plus a little bit more. Once this is attained, there is nothing left to strive for. You are the best, after all.

For the customary loser, it leads to the creation of an idol: the winner. The loser now becomes a chronic underachiever. With no hope of "winning," there is nothing left to strive for. The winners and losers may have different journeys, but they arrive at the same endpoint: inertia.

It creates animosity. God's best for you is constant, predetermined when you were created. A fellow competitor's best is variable, characterized by good days and bad days. Once you stop competing with yourself, suddenly, there's an easier way to become the best. Why not create strategic "bad days," for the competition?

The beautiful thing is that you really don't have to learn anything new to win. Just intimidate, slander, viciously hurt, oppress, and ultimately permanently silence everyone else. If the losers are injured and hate your guts, so what? Losers don't count. The ultimate prize is to be the best among other people, isn't it?

It creates pride. The winner really starts to believe his or her own hype. Statements such as, "I'm the best you've got" or, "Thank God I am so blessed compared to Mr. X or Ms. Y," start to become a permanent fixture in conversation, and a Pharisee is born.

The loss of humility leads to blindness, a blindness to learning, especially from "inferior people." To keep up the appearance of being "all-knowing," learning now becomes an expression of weakness and is shunned. The longer this state of affairs persists, the bigger the mythical reputation of invincibility grows and learning becomes even harder.

It creates shame. Eventually, mistakes made pile up to the point that things fall apart in a tangible, visible way. Everybody gets to see the end result of the mistakes made but ignored, of the lies told, and the self deception sold.

Put on the whole armor of God... Stand therefore, having your loins girt about with truth. Ephesians 6:11, 14.

The belt of truth always holds up your pants. Sooner or later with lies, your pants fall to your ankles, and privates become generals. Hidden matters become available for general inspection, and the public ruthlessly gorges itself on the sordid details.

Usually in these matters, the individual is torn down to even lower than what they are. This leads to the phenomenon of shame: the state of a spirit functioning below its station.

It creates isolation. God created community, a manifestation of his love and a fruit of his joy. Shame comes with a terrible consequence, one for which mankind was not designed: isolation, the direct antithesis of what God's community is all about. It is for this reason that Isaiah describes shame as the functional opposite of joy.

Therefore thus saith the Lord GOD, Behold, my servants shall eat, but ye shall be hungry: behold, my servants shall drink, but ye shall be thirsty: behold, my servants shall rejoice, but ye shall be ashamed. Isaiah 65:13.

Shame is the common end point of a bruised spirit. Shame happened to Adam and Eve after they ate the forbidden fruit, causing them to hide from God. It happened to Cain after he murdered his brother Abel, turning him into a vagabond. It has happened to many a politician and celebrity, causing him or her to hide in a rehabilitation clinic.

As you can see, shame is followed by an instinctual, almost knee-jerk reaction to run and hide one's self away. But that is no real surprise. It is just Satan's way of separating you from other people. I told you earlier: Satan puts asunder what God has put together.

It creates destruction. If isolation persists long enough—especially if the isolated individual willfully hides away from God—destruction ensues. The spirit is starved and dies and the whole body is lost. There is nothing worse in creation than sin-induced isolation. It separates you from God and life.

And so it goes, the strange, sinister sequence of competing against one another. This has been a bedrock of Satan's attack on mankind, from the foundations of the world. It is responsible for racism and tribalism—"micro-racism"—between different tribes of a common race.

It is responsible for most of the vicious massacres done in the name of religion over the years. It accounts for religious sectarianism, including the attitude of various denominations within the Christian church. It causes strife within families, ill feeling with neighbors, and breaks in friendships. Yet, it has been legitimized as a normal part of life.

Our sports industry is built around this unhealthy practice: "Get in their heads! They'll crack under pressure! You ain't got nothin'!" Denigrating slogans routinely are used to make opponents have a "bad day" and lose. Sometimes, even more sinister techniques are employed. Yet we spend exorbitant amounts of time, money, and emotional energy to authenticate this behavior, rubber-stamping it as a normal fact of life.

The red flag should be how much money these athletes earn. Why on earth should a fully grown man in a pair of tight pants hit a ball with a stick and earn two hundred and fifty million dollars over five years, while a teacher who grooms the next generation of mankind cannot earn that amount of money in one hundred and fifty years of continuous teaching?

How can a person run a piece of pigskin for one hundred yards and earn millions a year, while a nurse who extends loving care to people at their most vulnerable, not earn this amount in her whole nursing career, even if she retired at seventy?

Such glaring anomalies should prompt the question: Why? Why does so much money get poured into these pleasant and yet, not exactly vital, life activities? Because Satan has a huge investment in propagating this type of competition.

Satan, the deceiver of this earth, heartily backs projects that forward his evil purposes on earth. After all, once learned, such attitudes will be used to destroy other people and eventually oneself in much more meaningful arenas, such as the pathway to God.

Here's a thought: If a Muslim and a Christian were both interested in finding heaven, but refrained from competing against each other, maybe they would be looking at the functional results of their individual beliefs. If there was a more real result, it would win the day, for the true pilgrim of truth. If there was no "I'm better than you" syndrome, there would be no shame in having believed the wrong thing for so long.

Maybe, there would be a better chance of assimilating the truth, rather than clinging doggedly to dogmatic doctrine, just to avoid being made to feel small and inferior. Maybe there would be a guilt-free change in position to the real truth, by people who hunger for true righteousness, exposing the wicked individuals who use religious doctrine as a smokescreen, to glorify themselves: individuals who are erroneously classified as Christians or Muslims when they are, in reality, neither.

What if this wicked group of people who sneak under the umbrella of various religions were grouped together under a special name: the megalomaniacs? Could Saddam and Hitler, Stalin and Napoleon, all be honorary members of this new faith? Just a thought.

So, what do we do? We are hard-wired to compete!

We must restore competition to its true, original meaning.

Think of your body as three parts—spirit, mind, and body—all striving *together* as one for the prize of God's best for our lives. This prize is grasped by faith in the gospel of reconciliation to our maker through our Messiah, Jesus Christ.

Only let your conversation be as it becometh the gospel of Christ: that whether I come and see you, or else be absent, I may hear of your affairs, that ye stand fast in one spirit, with one mind striving together for the faith of the gospel. Philippians 1:27.

Did you see it? Several people *competing* for the prize of reconciling to God and inheriting his kingdom *in harmony*, as was originally intended. Learn how to compete by watching babies and young children develop new skill sets. They serve as practical guides on healthy competition. I watch my young sons develop and clearly see God's design in the kingdom of heaven.

For laziness, redefine the prize. The target needs to be God's best for *you*, not some other person's best. The only one who truly knows your best is God himself. So, constantly discuss with him about your performance in any given situation. God loves to hear your voice; it makes him smile.

Keep honing your abilities, constantly checking with him. He answers! You will know when you have maxed out in that area; you will have a peaceful, completed feeling about your spirit, not the restless, fidgety, sometimes empty feeling that comes after the euphoria of defeating an opponent wears off.

For animosity, apologize and make restitution with works. If you have animosity against your competitor, repent to God and tear up the marker you have imagined they owe you. It sets you free more than it does your detractors.

If your competitor has animosity against you, repent to God for the part you played in making them sin. Apologize, if possible, to the hurt individual. If it turns out that the animosity is totally unjustified, God will help your detractor see that. He made them; God knows better than anyone else how to correct them.

Saying you are sorry alone, however, does not cut it. You have to also show you are sorry by works. This involves tangible activities which yield the fruit of repentance. As we have seen already, the kingdom of heaven is dynamic, defined by its functional activity. Actions really do speak louder than words. Zacchaeus used the technique of restitution of works, and obtained salvation for him and his household.

And Zacchaeus stood, and said unto the Lord; Behold, Lord, the half of my goods I give to the poor; and if I have taken anything from any man by false accusation, I restore him fourfold. Luke 19:8.

And Jesus said unto him, This day is salvation come to this house, forasmuch as he also is a son of Abraham. Luke 19:9.

Jesus' response was a direct result of Zacchaeus' apology-in-action. He was blessed with the coveted title of being a son of Abraham. Was he a descendant of Abraham before his restitution? Yes.

However, Abraham is held up as the epitome of faith in Scripture. I believe Jesus used that title at that instant because, functionally, Zacchaeus was finally acting like it.

For pride, seek humility. Most people do not consider themselves proud. A useful self-assessment tool is a two-part test: What new life techniques did I apply this week? What do I value more, statements about how well I am doing, or statements that teach me to be better than I already am?

If the answer is "none" to the first question and you value compliments over teaching, you are proud. Humility is the lifelong student who applies what he learns, but is always hungry for more knowledge.

Be a hungry student of God. Speedily and enthusiastically carry out practical exercises delivered to you by your divine teacher, the Holy Spirit. Gobble up his Word, the spirit of Jesus Christ.

Blessed are they which do hunger and thirst after righteousness: for they shall be filled. Matthew 5:6.

For shame and isolation, seek courage and repentance. Basically: "'Fess up." This takes courage, but it has to be done to be a recipient of God's way out. God has a secret weapon to help keep shamed spirits from taking that lonely desolate road of isolation and, ultimately, self-destruction: his throne of grace.

Let us therefore come boldly unto the <u>throne of grace</u>, that we may obtain mercy, and find grace to help <u>in time of need</u>. Hebrews 4:16.

Cain only needed to ask God for his forgiveness and he would have been fine. The same went for Adam and Eve, who never once in the Bible asked for God to have mercy on them, unlike King David when he sinned. David wrote a whole song about his repentance: Psalm 51.

In fact, humans from the days of Cain's curse kept isolating themselves from God for at least one hundred and five more years—from Seth's birth to the birth of his son Enos—before they finally started calling on the name of the Lord. And to think: God's hand was outstretched the whole time!

There is no antidote for destruction.

LAST WORDS

It seems fitting to end by showcasing two stories, one ancient and the other recent, that can be used as vignettes on the potentially damaging effect of the "I am better than you" syndrome—especially when results do not line up to the satisfaction of the would-be winner.

Cain was competing with Abel. He could not accept that he had more to learn in the area of godly sacrifice than his brother, being the elder brother and all. This explains his anger toward Abel, who had nothing to do with the Cain's offering. It was an anger so intense that *Cain took his brother out to the field and slew him* (Genesis 4:3-8, adapted).

Ireland produced one of the greatest upsets in cricket World Cup history, beating Pakistan by three wickets in a rain-interrupted Group D match Saturday and consigning the 1992 champions to a first-round exit.— Associated Press, March 18, 2007.

Ireland produced one of the greatest victories in cricket's rich history by beating Pakistan on St. Patrick's Day amid unbelievable tension in Jamaica—Oliver Brett, BBC SPORT, March 17, 2007.

The genteel sport of cricket was dealt a brutal blow when Jamaican police said Pakistan's national coach was murdered in his hotel room a day after his team suffered a humiliating World Cup loss.—Associated Press, March 23, 2007.

THE LIZARD'S GAMBIT

T he cat was hungry. It had been two hours since his last
snack.

He was very grateful to the huge but nice two-legged
animal that took him in, regularly fed him gourmet cat
snacks, and insisted that, from time to time, he drink milk
from its great, cupped paw.

He had a two-room apartment that was warm and cozy. It
was enclosed in a gigantic multi-partitioned stadium that the
huge two-legged creature, along with two other, even bigger
two-legged beasts, called "home." His benefactor called
them Mum and Dad, but from what he could see, they were
obviously servants of some sort. His friend was clearly the
boss, which was all well and good, because he wasn't so sure
about those other two. He sometimes caught them giving
him a dirty look.

Oh, yeah, he was living the life. Yet every now and then,
as he strolled through the neighborhood, he felt a familiar
tug in his gut, a throw back to his ghetto childhood days. His
benefactor would be shocked if it found out that, every now
and then, he slipped up and ate "street meat." His stomach
rumbled.

He sniffed the air, smelling a familiar aroma: food. His
whiskers twitched expectantly, all his carnivorous instincts
primed for instant action. He edged closer to his target with

cat-like stealth, toward an unsuspecting target: a lizard, sun-bathing languorously, on a ledge.

The cat tensed, generating speed and power in its haunches, and struck before the suddenly terrified lizard had time to think, "Abort ledge!" Gotcha! Triumph, however, soon gave way to confusion. Suddenly there were two lizards! The cat was momentarily stunned. How did that happen? Well, he couldn't chase them both; he already had one alive, so he'd let the other one slide for today. Besides, the fleeing lizard had quite a head start, and the cat's stamina wasn't what it used to be.

So, he settled down to play a little with his vigorously wriggling lizard. He liked to do a little exercise before meals; he'd read somewhere it was good for the heart. Three minutes later, his "lizard" had stopped wriggling. He looked at it with disgust. "Three minutes, is that all you've got? Dead already?" The thrill was gone; the whole attraction was "live" street meat.

"Oh, well." He disinterestedly strolled away. *Meow.* "Enough excitement for one day. Home, sweet home, here I come," he thought, as he retraced his steps down well-known streets, his hunger pangs temporarily forgotten.

Three minutes away, the "other" lizard was still running, putting distance between himself and the cat, frightened half to death, but through it all, wearing a self-satisfied little smirk.

You'd better be careful; you got lucky again with that tail-breaking parlor trick, but you'll need to lay low until you grow another tail. Thank God for cheap parlor tricks and dumb cats. Works every time.

BROKEN HOME

❖

All spirits give instructions.
Being human means having a body, soul, and spirit.
The human spirit receives instructions from other spirits.
The human spirit was made to be indwelled by God.

Why do we like our homes so much? We get this relaxed, warm fuzzy feeling when after a hard day's work, we go home. It's as if there's a tracking device that draws us to the couch, keeps us in a stupor in front of the TV, an irresistible pull to the dining room table or my personal favorite, the pantry. I'm feeling better already, just talking about it!

We all are wired with that "homing" device. Home may not be the biggest, the fanciest or, let's face it, the neatest place in town, but it is by far the most personal. If there's junk, it's my junk, thank you very much! If I choose to keep a one-eared ceramic rabbit in my front yard to confuse the real bunnies, that's my business.

My home is my sanctuary, where I can just *be*.

We all can relate to this truth; it's *visceral*. But what about God? When it comes to home, how is he wired?

Actually, God likes his home too.

God chose his own home—it isn't the fanciest, the biggest, or the most majestic looking, but make no mistake, it is the dearest place in the world to him. Where's it located? Suffice it to say, God's home is not where we have thought it was.

Let's piece together the story. God made everything in the universe, fierce, delicate, big, small, etc. Then God decided he wanted to build a home for himself. He loves to see and oversee all the majestic wonders of the universe, but he also wants to kick back and relax in his own crib.

So, he picked a parcel of land and made himself a home. The parcel of land is actually called heaven and earth. Surprise! You thought heaven was his home! Not really: Heaven is part of his *house*; it's the executive wing, actually. The earth also is a part of his house. In fact, God rests his royal toes on it.

Thus saith the LORD, The heaven is my throne, and the earth is my footstool. Isaiah 66:1.

A house is just a shell to showcase your home.

His home is where the real goodies live—the memories, the power, the relationships, the very *essence* of him; that's the Almighty's sweet spot. Or, put another way, God's home is his place of glory and rest.

So, where is God's home? You really don't have to look very far to find it. In fact, it has been under our noses the whole time. *It's you.*

Well, that's a surprise! We are not the most imposing creatures in the universe, but that's hardly the point! We were always the home God chose for himself. In fact, it was the reason we were made in the first place.

And God said, Let us make man in our image. Genesis 1:26.

So, there you have it. Your home is made in your own image. So is God's. You rest and glory in your home. So does God. Your skinny shanks and pot belly may not fit the "streets of gold" mental image you've carried around of God's dwelling place. But then again, your home isn't St. Paul's Cathedral either, is it?

I know, it feels a little weird to be a living, walking, talking mobile home for the creator of the universe, but it's really not that strange, if you think about it for a minute.

What's home for you? Your family, your pets, even sometimes your pests, human ones inclusive. These are expressed in all sorts of ways: pictures, phone messages, the pitter-patter of young feet, muddy flip flops, the welcoming bark of a dog, etc. A lot of what constitutes home for you is *anchored in living things*.

Inanimate objects alone do not showcase the glory of life; therefore, if life defines God's character, he cannot be fully expressed in inanimate places.

Howbeit the most High dwelleth not in temples made with hands. Acts 7:48.

Where is the house that ye build unto me? and where is the place of my rest? For all those things hath mine hand made... saith the LORD: <u>but to this man will I look</u>, even to him that is poor and of a contrite spirit. Isaiah 66:1-2.

The truth is that heaven is a cool pad and earth's a nice extension, but it's all kind of *cramped*. It can't contain all of God's treasured stuff. So, he puts all the real goodies in you instead.

Now, here's an intriguing question: God gave the first humans instructions to be fruitful and multiply, filling the earth, in the Book of Genesis (Gen. 1:28). Why did God choose an increasing vehicle such as mankind to express himself?

God needs *that many* living humans to fully express his character.

This is a mind-boggling number of human souls. Remember the discussion about the soul, your medical mind, the part of you that ultimately defines you as *you*? There never have been two identical souls. Never. Just like there never has been a thumbprint like yours, even if you're an identical twin.

We are talking about an unimaginable number of aspects or "faces" to God's character. Do you see why heaven structurally cannot contain him? Heaven and "the heaven of heavens," as Solomon so eloquently put it, can't quite cut it as a home.

But who is able to build him an house, seeing the heaven and heaven of heavens cannot contain him? who am I then, that I should build him an house, save only to burn sacrifice before him? 2 Chronicles 2:6.

Now having broadened our view of the magnitude of God, let us reexamine the concept of Jesus Christ the man once again. While each of us was made to highlight several different aspects of God, Jesus Christ expresses the full kit and caboodle of God's glory.

For to one is given by the Spirit the word of wisdom; to another the word of knowledge by the same Spirit; To another faith by the same Spirit; to another the gifts of healing. 1 Corinthians 12:8-10.

Beware lest any man spoil you through philosophy... and not after Christ. For in him dwelleth <u>all the fulness of the Godhead</u> bodily. Colossians 2:8-9.

How magnificent a person can that be? Only the one whose spirit is made up of every word God has ever said. God's words, in turn, say precisely who he is. We learn about the faces of God by learning from the one who embodies all of God's faces.

He that hath seen me has seen the Father. John 14:9.

Come unto me, all ye that labour and are heavy laden, and I will give you rest... Take my yoke upon you, and <u>learn of me</u>. Matthew 11:28-29.

Looking at these statements about Jesus and mankind reveals a hidden truth: We learn God's character from facets we see *in each other*, facets that are identical to the character of Jesus Christ revealed in Scripture! "Each other" includes *every* person, of *every* race, and *every* color. Look at this passage from the Book of Isaiah, juxtaposed against Jesus' comments to his disciples in the Book of John.

The God of <u>the whole earth</u> shall he be called... And <u>all thy children</u> shall be <u>taught</u> of the LORD. Isaiah 54:5-12.

At that day ye shall know that <u>I am in my Father</u>, and <u>ye in me</u>, and <u>I in you</u>. John 14:20.

God's character traits are, therefore, seen in humans all over planet earth. How much we learn depends on how many people we critically observe. You, therefore, have a mandate to be a social butterfly. Learn from people of all shades and colors with objectivity, free of prejudice. Do not think you are God's only gift to mankind; in other words, don't attempt to make God a liar. Don't you know that the glory of God is man, that the Lord's glory fills the *whole* earth, and that God never lies?

For a man indeed ought not to cover his head, forasmuch as he is the image and glory of God. 1 Corinthians 11:7.

Holy, holy, holy, is the LORD of hosts: the whole earth is full of his glory. Isaiah 6:3.

It was impossible for God to lie. Hebrews 6:18.

With this new perspective, a lot of Bible statements suddenly take on a new dimension of clarity, a straightforward sensibleness not seen before.

Decisions we make on earth automatically are made in heaven; a throne is where a king's decisions are executed.

The LORD God formed every beast of the field, and every fowl of the air... and whatsoever Adam called every living creature, that was the name thereof. Genesis 2:19.

Whatsoever ye shall bind on earth shall be bound in heaven: and whatsoever ye shall loose on earth shall be loosed in heaven. Matthew 18:18.

Our feet pad around on the earth; the earth is God's footstool, after all.

How beautiful are the feet of them that preach the gospel of peace, and bring glad tidings of good things! Romans 10:15.

Every place whereon the <u>soles of your feet</u> shall tread shall be yours. Deuteronomy 11:24.

And, believe it or not, Jesus called us little versions of God—or gods.

Jesus answered them, Is it not written in your law, I said Ye are gods? John 10:34.

I have said, Ye are gods; and all of you are children of the most High. Psalm 82:6.

Why is understanding man as God's home so important? Because the information we have just learned highlights a startling truth about God.

God was always going to come in mankind.

This is why Adam was created in God's image and the spirit of God was breathed into Adam: God in man. This is why Jesus kept calling himself the Son of man, in this case meaning he would come forth from humans, as God's words of instruction. Or, simply, "the Word."

And because ye are <u>sons</u>, God hath sent forth the Spirit of his <u>Son</u> into your hearts. Galatians 4:6.

And they shall call his name Emmanuel, which being interpreted is, God with us. Matthew 1:23.

Emmanuel: the ridiculously simple truth that has been the seat of religious controversy, for eons.

In Judaism, the name of God is so sacred that traditionally it is not uttered for fear of death. The Judaic faith does not believe in the fullness of God coming in man. In their minds, mankind is too stinky for that. It is why the Jews of Jesus' time tried to kill him.

The Jews answered him, saying, For a good work we stone thee not, but for blasphemy; and because that <u>thou, being a man, makest thyself God</u>. John 10:33.

Therefore the Jews sought the more to kill him, because he not only had broken the Sabbath, but said also that <u>God was his Father, making himself equal with God</u>. John 5:18.

The Muslim faith also looks favorably on the concept of divinely appointed prophets, including Jesus Christ. However, God in man? Nope. It is why the ceremonial dome that sits to this day on the temple mount in Jerusalem, the site of Solomon's and later on Herod's temple, a dome that was made by Muslims in 691 A.D., bears the inscription: *It is not for God to take a son.*

These two religions had a much deeper understanding of what it meant to be called a son than we do today. It meant you came forth from your father and were, in fact, for all functional purposes, your father. This was too much for either religion to swallow. This was at the core of the Jesus Christ controversy.

But in the Christian faith, man is God's home. The home cannot rest without its owner, and the owner cannot rest in his home. Something is terribly wrong with God's home. It has not been ready to receive him.

And Jesus said unto him, Foxes have holes, and birds of the air have nests: but the Son of man hath not where to lay his head. Luke 9:58.

Come on to me, all ye that labour and are heavy laden, and I will give <u>you rest</u>. Matthew 11:28.

A person without God is a broken home.

What a tragedy! So, God is currently in the business of restoring his broken mobile homes. He is not working on making a blueberry more blue.

But Jesus answered them, My Father worketh hitherto, and I work. John 5:17.

How did this tragedy happen? Earlier on, we discussed the fall of man in the Garden of Eden. God had been the first gardener of this indescribably beautiful place before his two mobile homes came along to do the same job. However, remember the forbidden fruit thing? On the day that the fruit was eaten, as the Word of God had said, the man and woman both died. On that day, God's spiritual home was broken.

Now, the big question is: Could man's spirit be dead and yet, he appears as if he is alive? Let's backtrack a little.

God breathed into man to make him alive. God's living breath made man *a living soul.*

And the LORD God formed man of the dust of the ground, and breathed into his nostrils the breath of life; and man became a living soul. Genesis 2:7.

So, it is fair to say, without the breath or spirit of God, man was not living. Adam died spiritually when he ate the fruit. But Adam "lived" long after this time, had sons and daughters and finally "died," at the age of nine hundred and thirty years.

And the days of Adam after he had begotten Seth were eight hundred years: and he begat sons and daughters: And all the days that Adam lived were nine hundred and thirty years: and he died. Genesis 5:4-5.

So, given what we know, let's revisit the question: Could man's spirit be dead and yet, he appears as if he is alive? *The answer is yes.*

A broken home actually is a dead man walking. Much like the severed lizard's tail, Adam created an ocular deception by wriggling around for three minutes. Three minutes, after which it became clear that the lizard's tail was dead. Adam and Eve's disobedience created a disturbing characteristic in their descendants: humans.

We are born dead. But our "wriggle time," on average, lasts 78 years here in the U.S.

Dead spirit, dead man. It is that simple. It doesn't matter whether he is on the dust, or in the dust. Jesus Christ said as much. He kept calling Abraham, Isaac, and Jacob living.

Have ye not read that which was spoken... I am the God of Abraham, and the God of Isaac, and the God of Jacob? God is not the God of the dead, but of the living. Matthew 22:31-32.

But these three individuals were quite clearly, to the Jewish people's eyes, very, very dead.

Art thou greater than our father Abraham, which is dead? and the prophets are dead: whom makest thou thyself? John 8:53.

Here's another scenario: A man who had followed Jesus Christ as a disciple had a piece of serious business to take care of, or so he imagined: the business of burying his father. Jesus, however, had a *slightly* different take on the order of business for the day.

But he said, Lord, suffer me first to go and bury my father. Jesus said unto him, Let the dead bury their dead: but go thou and preach the kingdom of God. Luke 9:59-60.

Whom was Jesus calling the dead? The man's dead father, and presumptively the dead man's relatives and friends! "Walking" dead; "about to be buried" dead, it made no difference; dead is dead.

So, can this tragic state of affairs be fixed? Who will fix God's broken home? The homeowner will.

God knows exactly how his home is supposed to look.

Our spirits are known, and have been known to God a long, long time. Long before our bodies showed up on earth, because our individual spirits were made during the six days of creation. God has *finished* creating the heavens and the earth.

Then the word of the LORD came unto me saying, Before I formed thee in the belly I knew thee; and before thou camest forth out of the womb I sanctified thee, and I ordained thee a prophet unto the nations. Jeremiah 1:4-6.

Thine eyes did see my substance, yet being unperfect; and in thy book all my members were written, which in continuance were fashioned, when as yet there was none of them. Psalm 139:16.

He is not making new humans every minute of every day. However, due to Adam's mistake, man is conceived spiritually dead. And he only awakens when the Holy Spirit of God enters the person and raises that individual up from death. Remember? The Holy Spirit is the activator of all life systems, wherever they exist.

The Holy Spirit delivers life.

The Holy Spirit's job is to carry the instructional blueprint of life in the universe and *actually make it happen.* Hence, that human's spirit cannot stay dead. This is what is meant by spiritual rebirth, or becoming "born again." Jesus Christ was conceived in the womb *by the Holy Spirit*; therefore, Jesus' spirit was alive at his conception.

That which is conceived in her is of the Holy Ghost...
and thou shalt call his name JESUS: for he shall save his
people from their sins. Matthew 1:20-21.

So, God's redemption plan unfolded. Jesus Christ went through the growing-up processes common to all people, literally showcasing God's home. But even Jesus' spirit died. Remember his heart wrenching cry, *"My God, my God, why hast thou forsaken me?"* during his crucifixion? That was when Jesus' spirit died and was separated from his Father. With that cry, Jesus fulfilled all aspects of the human condition.

And as it is appointed unto men once to die, but after this
the judgment. Hebrews 9:27.

For both he that sanctifieth (Jesus) and they who are
sanctified (humans) are all of one: for which cause he

is not ashamed to call them brethren. Hebrews 2:11, adapted.

Why is this so important? As God's Son, he is the inheritor of God's kingdom. However, only *mankind* can inherit the kingdom of God—not angels, nor animals, but the sons and daughters of men.

What is man, that thou art mindful of him? ... Thou madest him to have dominion over the works of thy hands; thou has put <u>all things</u> under his feet. Psalm 8:4-6.

And man must be born twice to even enter God's kingdom. Obviously, he has to enter the kingdom to inherit it.

Verily, verily I say unto thee, Except a man be born of water and of the Spirit, he cannot enter into the kingdom of God. John 3:5.

The part of this statement that traditionally has garnered a lot of attention has been being born of the spirit. However, you have to be born once, to be born again.

You need to be born of the flesh as well, which, given the context of Jesus' discussion with Nicodemus, was the "born of water" part of the discussion. Not water baptism, but rather, the traditionally called "bag of waters," or amniotic fluid, that bathes a baby *in utero* and is necessary for normal development to term.

This is the "my water broke!" phenomenon, romantically depicted as representative of the onset of labor by secular media. Even test-tube babies are kept in artificial amniotic fluid or "a beaker of waters" for development into a normal-term child.

Therefore, Jesus Christ, the Son of God, through whom all things were created, was destined to pass through this same physical birthing process to inherit the kingdom of God. You had to be a man or woman—*mankind*, generically—to inherit the kingdom of heaven. God is absolutely consistent, and his only begotten Son was not exempt from that rule.

What is man, that thou art mindful of him?... thou crownedst him with glory and honour, and didst set him over the works of thy hands: Thou has put all things in subjection under his feet. Hebrews 2:7.

But we see Jesus... crowned with glory and honour... For it became him, for whom are all things, and by whom are all things... For both he that sanctifieth and they who are sanctified are all of one. Hebrews 2:9-11.

Jesus Christ coming as a man solved the broken home dilemma, once and for all, for all humans. But each person has to choose God's fix, which I'll be the first to admit may feel awkward at first. A dead man walking usually doesn't know he's dead—until he really starts living.

Choose life, that both thou and thy seed may live. Deuteronomy 30:19.

LAST WORDS

How many times have you thought of yourself as a container for life, as Jesus did? That is primarily how he thought of himself, and acted accordingly. So should we. However, the tragedy, the real tragedy of the human condition, is that *we have not understood who we are.*

Jesus himself told his disciples at one point, "You don't know of whose spirit you are." Then again, there is this sorrowful eloquence, a poignant lament from a wise and—at the point of its telling, old—King Solomon.

Folly is set in great dignity, and the rich sit in low place. I have seen servants upon horses, and princes walking as servants upon the earth. Ecclesiastes 10:6-7.

SPIRIT LESSONS (conclusion)

Being human means having a body, soul, and spirit.
The human spirit receives instructions from other spirits.
Jesus Christ's spirit is a book of all of God the Father's instructions.
Jesus Christ is, therefore, different from all other men. Through him, paradise lost was found, and the human spirit can now be instructed and indwelled by God.
This is the kingdom of God.
The lessons on the human spirit end here.

SECTION III

NO WONDER, NO WONDER

The other day when I was thinking
Of Almighty Father God
And Jesus Christ, My only Savior
The Holy Spirit, Moses' rod

There came a question to my being
One that wouldn't go away;
If God's the same today and always
Where's that mighty rod today?

God made that rod grow buds that wither
Made it turn into a snake
Had it split the Red Sea open
To across His people take.
Moses knew the power in it
Was from God, not his own hands,
Obedience to God's direction
Would lead to Promised Lands.

A stiff-necked people, prone to murmur
Never made it to that place.
Though God provided food and water
Clothes of wear showed not a trace.

Now '06 is ending
In this nation where I live
And its people rich, protected,
Won't to God the credit give.

Much less obey the Law He's given
Or trust upon his Grace
This must be why His power's missing,
Of the rod, is not a trace.

Michael W. Reed
December 2006

THE ARGUMENT

※

Here's a story of an argument. A couple of body parts were involved in a vigorous exchange about who was the greatest. Actually, the eye kind of started it all. He'd been going hard at it now for the last ten minutes, with his favorite "debate" partner, the heart.

"Now, without me, you can't see a thing. I rest my case." Smugly he settled back into his socket.

The heart snorted. "You've gotta be kiddin' me! *You* can't see a thing, if I don't pump you blood, food, oxygen, all the good stuff! Without me, you'd be blind as a bat!"

The eye leaned forward, bulging out of his weary socket once again. "Come on, Artie, let's be real. Without me, sure you get to pump—all the way into a ditch! I don't mean to brag, but you *know* who really keeps things moving around here." Suddenly he looked nervously upwards, toward the brain. "That is, except for the boss man over here. Right, Brother Brian?"

"Keep me out of this argument."

"All right, boss, I understand." The eye, cutting a glance over at the heart, was unable to resist one last dig. "The boss can't pick favorites publicly, but you and I know the truth, right?"

"Hey, hey! Can you keep it down? I'm trying to catch some sleep over here!" An irritated appendix turned over on his side and pulled the bed sheets over his head.

The eye, ever ready for a new challenge and not in the least bit sleepy, promptly fired back. "Oh, be quiet and go to sleep. After all, you aren't good for anything else!" As Penny the appendix sat up glaring at him, he laughed gleefully. "Don't look at me like that!"

The glare got fiercer. "I'm really starting to get upset, now. Don't push me, or I'll explode!"

The other body organs had been only half listening to the eye's never-ending argument, but suddenly they perked up. This was infinitely more interesting. Penny the appendix was the wild child. Maybe he was just the one to shut up that old bossy eye.

"C'mon, Penny! Go for it!" And then, giggling and dancing the cabbage patch: *"Don't push me, 'cause I'm close to the edge!"*

A restless sigh from the colon: *Here we go again.*

"You all need to just let Penny be, OK? Stop aggravating him!" And then, with a nervous look over at the appendix: "OK, Penny, settle down. Go to sleep."

But Penny was having none of it. "Oh, no! It's on, now! Let's see how important you all are, when I explode!"

Legs got in on the act. Trying to smooth things over, she strolled over to the fridge. "Anybody want a drink? Iced tea, maybe? I'll get it." Then, as an afterthought: "You know, come to think of it, I'm the only one who actually *gets* stuff around here. That makes me your Mama." Turning to hands, she adopted a waiting pose. "Give me a hand here, will you?"

But hands folded themselves together, giving the new diva an arch look. "Oh, no! Do it yourself, Mama! After all, you're the only one that actually *gets* stuff around here. Hah! Who's your Mama now, hmm?"

That was when the quiet one decided to help matters. He timidly sat up on his "bottom" bunk bed. His name is Pluto and he lives out back, where the bowels end and the sun doesn't shine.

"Maybe we should…"

The eye and several other body parts turned toward Pluto and laughed disdainfully.

"Oh, you've got a voice too, garbage disposal?"

"If anybody should be quiet, it should be you."

"Shut up!"

So, Pluto shut up.

Seven days later, murmurs of panic were heard from various organs.

"Oh, no!"

"Pluto's gone postal!"

"We know Penny's crazy, but who would have thought that quiet little Pluto…"

"Eye and heart, why are you two always stirring up stuff, huh?

EYE (*Blearily*): Leave me alone. I just wanna curl up in a corner and die!

STOMACH: This house stinks! And the gas! Sweet Moses! I think I'm gonna puke!

MOUTH: Oh, no! Please don't! I just had a shower! Can't you hold it? Oh, all over my "pearly" shoes; what a mess!

KIDNEYS: This situation is out of control, you know what I'm sayin?' Brother Brian, do something!

BRAIN (mildly): Maybe you need to talk to Pluto. Apologize or something?

COLON: On behalf of all body parts we apologize to you, Pluto. You know what? How about (*pause, bloated burp*)… Excuse me, how about making you king, or queen, or whatever it takes to make you start talking?

WHAT IS THE CHURCH?
PART I: THE REVELATION

We all need one another. I know; it doesn't seem like it sometimes, but believe me, we do.

When you hear the word "church," what do you think it means?

Secular society usually identifies church by the buildings with the word "church" on them, and the people that congregate in those buildings, usually for up to a couple of hours, on Sundays.

If you go for the token hour or two a week, you are a "Christian" or "church-going person."

If you go more, you are "very religious."

If you go less, you are a "broad-minded Christian."

Whether you go or not, a public statement of belief in Jesus Christ spoken about once a decade or so labels you as an individual with a "private faith." I guess a more accurate description would be a "private faith briefly gone public," but then, what do I know?

Among the group of people who verbally identify themselves as Christians or followers of Jesus Christ, there is a different understanding of church.

Christians, all put together, constitute "the church."

"The church" congregates in a building titled "church," plus an alphabet soup of words.

There is a secret password to God's bedside telephone. It resides in the alphabet soup.

Individuals—Christian or not—who come to church are said to have been "churched."

Sometimes I think church people have more code words for each other than the CIA: Christian brother or sister; saints; serious Christians, "not a real" Christian; or, my personal espionage favorite, "undercover" Christians.

So, there you have it. Church buildings, church relatives, "connected" church, undercover church, and the churchy church goes to church to be churched, as apparently, church can be used as a noun, adjective, or verb.

Into these calm "church" waters I determinedly plunge, to give what I hope is God's perspective, from Scripture, on what church is.

But first of all, as usual, we have some spiritual work to do. Let's flesh out some spiritual perspectives.

When two spirits are directly connected together, they share instructions. However, they now also share their *minds:* hopes, dreams, feelings and plans, etc.

For what man knoweth the things of a man, save the spirit of man which is in him? even so the things of God knoweth no man, but the Spirit of God. 1 Corinthians 2:11.

Think of an internet blog. You sign on and post your thoughts on the blog in real time, thoughts now viewed by everyone else signed on to the same blog. The interaction is personal, as each blogger bares the workings of his mind to the other.

For who hath known the mind of the Lord, that he may instruct him? but we have the mind of Christ. 1 Corinthians 2:16.

Mixing of spirits leads to a meeting of the minds.

And before you start thinking dreamily about "happy hour" on Friday, I'm not talking alcohol here. People were designed to collectively show God's glory to all creation, with Jesus Christ being the complete embodiment of this glory. Each human mind is designed to show some aspects of Jesus' mind. Indeed, collectively, we should have the mind of Christ.

However, there is one small rider to being a part of this meeting, or mirroring of minds: We must love God.

Eye hath not seen, nor ear heard, neither have entered into the heart of man, the things which God hath prepared for them that love him. 1 Corinthians 2:9.

Loving God is learning about him and helping God achieve his greatest desire: to help *you!* The Father loves you; Jesus Christ embodies all God's instructions on how we can be helped.

For God so loved the world, that he gave his only begotten son, that whosoever believeth in him should not perish, but have everlasting life. John 3:16.

Loving God, therefore, means listening to and learning from Jesus. Below are excerpts of Jesus' words, encapsulating this very concept. The third excerpt is one of my favorite verses, in all Scripture.

If ye love me, keep my commandments. John 14:15.

My sheep hear my voice, and I know them, and they follow me. John 10:27.

Come unto me, all ye that labour and are heavy laden, and I will give you rest. Take my yoke upon you, and <u>learn of me</u>*; for I am meek and lowly in heart: and ye shall find rest unto your souls. For my yoke is easy, and my burden is light. Matthew 11:28-30.*

Whenever I read those last three verses, I feel *light*.

Therefore, for those who keep God's commandments, we are body parts designed to make up a whole body. Jesus Christ directs activities as the brain, or "Brother Brian" of the body. The body discussed here is a metaphor for something very special: It symbolizes Jesus Christ's church.

And he is the head of the body, the church. Colossians 1:18.

Jesus Christ's church is not just made up of Christians or Christ followers. Jesus attends his own church, too.

Jesus Christ's church is made up of Jesus and people, obeying God.

The word "church" actually comes from the root meaning "congregation," or "assembly." Now, given what we know of Jesus Christ's spirit, what do you think would define his church?

I am the way, the truth, and the life. John 14:6.

Life. Jesus Christ is life; therefore, his church has to be built with "living" fabric: an assembly or congregation of spiritually living people.

This is the living church. It is made of people, obeying God.

Is it possible that there is an assembly or congregation that might not be his? Let us look at these instructions from Jesus, in the Book of Matthew.

Upon this rock I will build my <u>church</u>; and the gates of hell shall not prevail against it. Matthew 16:18.

Jesus' church is built on the foundation of God's words—in other words, on Jesus himself. The foreman God the Father chose to supervise this particular building project was a man called Simon Peter.

This is the Peter of St. Peter's Cathedral fame. He used to be Simon Barjona, one of Jesus' disciples, but Jesus renamed him Peter, meaning "the rock." This predicted not only God's Word being the spiritual foundation of his church, but also Peter's supervisory role in the building of it.

They drank of <u>that spiritual Rock</u> that followed them: <u>and that Rock was Christ</u>. 1 Corinthians 10:4.

And I say also unto thee, That thou art <u>Peter</u>, and upon <u>this rock</u> I will build my church...And <u>I will give unto thee the keys</u> of the kingdom of heaven. Matthew 16:18-19.

Later on, Simon Peter stepped fully into this supervisory role, as his mantle of responsibility and actions are recorded in an exciting book of the Bible called the Acts of the Apostles.

But in the same Book of Acts, a certain young man filled with the Holy Spirit named Stephen used the term "church" to refer to Moses and the Israelites of Moses' time, the ones present at the parting of the Red Sea and the Exodus from Egypt.

This is he, that was in the <u>church</u> in the wilderness with the angel which spake to him in the mount Sina, and with our fathers... To whom our fathers would not obey, but thrust him from them. Acts 7:38-39.

Ye stiffnecked and uncircumcised in heart and ears, ye do always resist the Holy Ghost: as your fathers did, so do ye. Which of the prophets have not your fathers persecuted? Acts 7:51-52.

So, it would appear that church was a terminology that also applied to men of old—stubborn, contrary old men who lived prior to when Jesus walked the earth as a man. This is a church of disobedient people that persecute prophets.

A spirit is defined by its fruits; this is what is called the *dead church.* If the members of a church do not obey God's instructions and blueprint for life, they are dead. Therefore, we have the dead church, as well.

There is a dead church. It is made of people, disobeying God.

And unto the angel of the church in Sardis write... I know thy works, that thou hast a name that thou livest, and art dead. Revelation 3:1.

But she that liveth in pleasure is dead while she liveth. 1 Timothy 5:6.

The first statement is from Jesus to the church at a place called Sardis, the second from Paul, giving a word of caution to widows who do their own thing, rather than follow God's instructions.

Are there two churches—one living and the other dead? Not really. Dead and living are just adjectives of the assembly of people called church. They both are parts of one thing: that thing called church. So, what is church? Given what we know, church can only mean one thing.

"Church" means *people*.

WHAT IS THE CHURCH?
PART II: THE EXPLANATION

S urprise, surprise! The church is *people*! Let's dig into and explain this hidden—yet ridiculously simple—phenomenon.

The church is people: all people, including the first man, the first woman, and all their descendants. They are what is sometimes called the world. The church was formulated to spread its influence throughout the earth we live in. It was designed that way by our creator from the very beginning.

God is working to bring man from a post-fall situation to a pre-fall inheritance.

The ideal church is people, including Jesus Christ, obeying God. If that is the case, when was the first ideal church? When the first people obeyed God.

Adam and his wife were in the first church.

When Adam and his wife were made, Jesus was there. He started the grooming and preparation of the church at that time. This was pre-fall. It was the spirit of Jesus Christ who used to come down and chat with the first people, in the cool of the day.

And they heard the <u>voice</u> of the LORD God <u>walking</u> in the garden in the cool of the day. Genesis 3:8.

Now, Jesus Christ was not a man yet. Whether he appeared in man-like form, or the first people being alive spiritually could actually see his spirit moving from place to place, is not known. However, as sure as there is day and night, Jesus was *there*.

And so it was, until "the Adams" committed suicide. So, Jesus is building his second living church, out of the ashes of the first.

I am well aware of the traditionally held concept that the church was started by Peter in the First Century, having been foretold by Jesus Christ before his crucifixion. Well, let's hear what Peter the foreman had to say about the church in his own book.

But ye are a <u>chosen</u> generation, a royal priesthood, an holy nation, a <u>peculiar</u> people; that ye should shew forth the praises of him who hath called you out of darkness into his marvellous light. 1 Peter 2:9.

I underlined a couple of the adjectives; they are what make this group of people special. Look at the nouns they precede: generation. *People.* Don't you see it?

I understand that we have taken the church to be holy people, or holy buildings, or Christians who gather and formally worship God on Sunday or, in some cases, Saturday. This is partly true. But if this was the whole truth, several writings in the Scripture, large chunks of it, in fact, just don't add up.

The "people" concept of church is simple, but not easy to grasp. It took me a while to fully wrap my head around this truth myself. Like a lot of people I know, I used to think the same way about church as some of those earlier examples I gave at the beginning of this chapter.

All that until I read a snippet from the Book of Ephesians. That snippet kept nagging at me, like an unrelenting toothache. Let's look at the famous snippet, the description of Christ and the church, in the fifth chapter of Ephesians.

Husbands, love your wives, even as Christ also loved the church, and gave himself for it. Ephesians 5:25.

Here's my question: If the church only is composed of people in right standing with God, why would Jesus Christ have to lay down his life? Let's look at Jesus Christ's words, in the Gospels.

They that be whole need not a physician, but they that are sick... for I am not come to call the righteous, but sinners to repentance. Matthew 9:12-13.

Over the ages, many men have professed love to their spouses, punctuating it with the famous heart-melter, "I would lay down my life for you." However, very few men have had to put action to these words.

Would it be fair to say that a wife must be in dire straits to require this extreme measure of her husband?

The church must have been in serious trouble for Jesus Christ to lay down his life for it.

People who obey God are in right standing with him. Such people are not in trouble. Therefore, this group of individuals cannot be the sole composition of what is and has been called "church."

Christ died for the <u>ungodly</u>. Romans 5:6.

Husbands, love your wives, even as Christ also loved the church and gave himself for it; That he might sanctify and cleanse it with the washing of water by the word, That he might present it to himself a <u>glorious</u> church... holy and without blemish. Ephesians 5:25-27.

The church, therefore, cannot consist only of righteous people. There would be no reason for Jesus to die for it, to clean it up. The glorious church is the holy church achieved after the cleansing of a very dirty church. So, once again: What is the church, really?

Alleluia: for the Lord God omnipotent reigneth. Let us be glad and rejoice, and give honour to him: for the marriage of the Lamb is come and <u>his wife hath made herself ready</u>. Revelation 19:6-7.

And to her was granted that she should be arrayed in fine linen, clean and white: for the fine linen is <u>the righteousness of saints</u>. Revelation 19:8.

Typically at weddings, we identify a bride by what she is wearing. We also can see this from wedding pictures. However, she still is the chosen bride underneath all the clothing.

In this case, the righteousness of the saints is the clothing. So, strip away the clothes and we have a startling truth, once again: Saints without righteous clothes are *people*.

The church is people!

Now it makes sense. All you have to do is look around you. It is perfectly clear why this church needs saving. Let us examine Paul's perspective on the people that need saving, once again.

Husbands, love your wives, even as Christ also loved the church, and gave himself for it; That he might sanctify and cleanse it with the washing of water by the word, That he might present it to himself a glorious church... holy and without blemish... This is a great mystery: but I speak concerning Christ and the church. Ephesians 5:25-27, 32.

Now let's see what Paul wrote in another book, about four years later, to a young man named Titus.

For the grace of God that bringeth salvation hath appeared to <u>all men</u>, Teaching us that denying ungodliness and worldly lusts, we should live soberly, righteously, and godly, in this present world; Looking for that blessed hope, and the glorious appearing of the great God and our Saviour Jesus Christ: <u>Who gave himself for us</u>, that he might redeem us from all iniquity, and purify unto himself a <u>peculiar people</u>, zealous of good works. These things speak, and exhort, and rebuke with all authority. Let no man despise thee. Titus 2:11-15.

Did you catch it? Contextually, they are identical statements, describing whom Jesus Christ came to save and how he would do it. "The church" serves the same function in the Ephesian letter as "all men" serves, in the Titus letter.

Also note the way he ends the discussion in both letters. It is obvious that this teaching would encounter skepticism and resistance among professed Christian audiences.

This accounts for the somewhat placatory tone to the church at Ephesus. Look at the personal letter to Titus, written about four years later. Here, Paul indicates that this message, though truth, is not a popular one. It will be scoffed at but must be taught, highlighting its importance.

To be fair, on several occasions Paul called the Christians of his day "the church," which probably has led to people thinking it is an exclusive term, meant only for Christians. *Not so.* The same Paul, speaking to the "churches" at Galatia and Corinth, made it clear that with regards to entry into God's kingdom, there are only *two* groups: Those who would enter it, and those who would not, determined by who obeyed God's instructions and who didn't.

> *Adultery, fornication... lasciviousness, Idolatry, witchcraft, hatred... wrath, strife, seditions, heresies, Envyings... drunkenness, revellings... I have also told* <u>*you*</u> *in time past, that they which do such things shall not inherit the kingdom of God. Galatians 5:19-21.*

> *Know ye not that the unrighteous shall not inherit the kingdom of God? Be not deceived. 1 Corinthians 6:9.*

Unfortunately, Christians of the Twenty-First Century have divided people into *three* groups: the obedient church, the disobedient church, and the unbeliever, with the first two groups bound for the kingdom of heaven, albeit with different prizes when they get there. And the last group? Oh, well, these poor creatures have totally missed the boat.

This was not Paul's position.

Are we more accepting of Paul's teaching and the true meaning of the church than the First Century audience?

Well, let's just say that it is not exactly the most popular icebreaker in Christian gatherings.

In fact, most times I have mentioned this broadened definition of church to "Christian" audiences, the reception has ranged from distrust to frank rejection. I even have, on occasion, been regarded with the special wary look usually reserved for lunatics. Why is this so difficult a pill to swallow? Because it strips away an elitist mentality?

The body parts have spent too much time bickering with each other and missing the ultimate point: that they all bring a distinct skill set, but ultimately one plan. It is God's plan to make the dead church living.

Many body parts actually have ignored and discounted the brain, like the legs in the allegory above. Others have paid only lip service to the brain, using him as a tool to catapult them into an ascendant position of superiority, like the near incorrigible eye.

The light of the body is the eye... but when thine eye is evil, thy body also is full of darkness. Luke 11:34.

And if thy right eye offend thee, pluck it out, and cast it from thee. Matthew 5:29.

I guess the left eye is left, to do the job right.

But the brain, he knows how wonderful it could be if all body parts—each part unique and beautiful—were to function cohesively in an amazing display of perfect engineering under his wise direction. Yes, even the appendix, who models the part of God's kingdom that is all about God's rest, the "seventh day."

For God so loved the world, that he gave his only begotten Son. John 3:16.

Jesus Christ believes in that church so much, he gave himself for it. Once redeemed, the clothed church sounds very much like the following.

My soul shall be joyful in my God; for he hath clothed me with the garments of salvation, he hath covered me with the robe of righteousness...as a bride adorneth herself with her jewels. Isaiah 61:10.

It's a church worth saving.

WHAT IS THE CHURCH?
DEEPER THOUGHTS

※

The body can compensate for the absence of some organs, but two organs are indispensable.

God invites you to move within the whole mass of humanity-designated church to join the part that truly represents him: the living church, or the body of Christ.

Think about the body for a minute. You can live healthily without some organs such as "Penny" the appendix, the gall bladder, or the tonsils. You are disabled, but not vanquished, if you lose a hand, an eye, or some teeth. You can swap out just about every organ of the body by transplantation, such as the liver, heart, lungs, kidneys, even the corneas. All except for a couple of organs; the first one is the *brain*.

The brain represents Jesus Christ, the Rabbi.

Without the brain, it's a no-brainer; such is the pivotal role of Jesus Christ. A gangrenous body part can be cut out, and the body still lives. But a gangrenous brain? Sorry, pal.

I am the vine, ye are the branches: He that abideth in me, and I in him, the same bringeth forth much fruit: for <u>without me ye can do nothing</u>. John 15:5.

185

The brain is the first indispensable organ. What is the second one? *Blood.* This largely overlooked liquid organ carries nutrients to all other organs, without which, they die. Dead body parts do not have any blood supply. No blood, no oxygen or nutrient delivery. No nutrient delivery, no life. In the human body, therefore, blood is the activator of all life systems. Sound familiar?

Every moving thing that liveth shall be meat for you... But flesh with the life thereof, <u>which is the blood thereof,</u> shall ye not eat. Genesis 9:3-4.

Therefore I said unto the children of Israel, Ye shall eat the blood of no manner of flesh: for the life of all flesh <u>is</u> the blood thereof. Leviticus 17:14.

Sorry for messing up your rare steak dinner; please don't shoot the messenger. The food of the spirit is the Word or instructions of God. The same blood runs through all the organs, delivering the same food to each one. The same doctrine of Jesus Christ is carried through his church, delivered by the same Holy Spirit.

No man can say that Jesus is the Lord, but by the Holy Ghost. Now there are diversities of gifts, but the same Spirit. And there are differences of administrations, but the same Lord. 1 Corinthians 12:3-5.

Jesus therefore answered and said unto them ...I am that bread of life... Doth this offend you?...the words that I speak unto you, they are spirit, and they are life. John 6:43-63.

The blood represents the Holy Spirit.
The nutrients are Jesus Christ, the spirit.

The Word of God. Rip off a chunk of us and we should all be bloody, with the same blood, living off the same nutrients. We may not all perform the same actions, but we do all need to have the same nutrients—or doctrine.

Therefore, as much as we hate to hear it, there really is only one doctrinal position: Any other teaching about the church of Jesus Christ, the "my church" of Matthew 16, is a lie.

But though we, or an angel from heaven, preach any other gospel unto you than that which we have preached unto you, let him be accursed. Galatians 1:8.

Why such strong language from the apostle Paul in the passage above? Because any other doctrine deviates from life and kills people.

A dog's blood infused into a man will kill him. Blood poisoning—called septicemia, literally "bad blood"—kills too, and still is one of the leading causes of death today. Should a "dog blood" transfusion or septicemia be accursed? You bet.

It is, therefore, our responsibility to find out from the Holy Spirit the appropriate doctrinal position. How do we know it is the right doctrine? It must deliver what it promises. The measured outcomes or spiritual fruits will speak for themselves.

For a good tree bringeth not forth corrupt fruit; neither doth a corrupt tree bring forth good fruit. For every tree is known by his own fruit. Luke 6:43-44.

Interestingly, this same metaphor in God's church body applies to our own individual bodies. Remember: We are made in God's image and the principles of God's kingdom exist within us also.

In the same vein, persistently fruitless body parts are ultimately pruned off God's church, leaving only the living members, with Jesus Christ as head. The same rules apply to us as individuals, in the area of unfruitful habits and behaviors. Look at these two verses from Jesus.

I am the true vine, and my Father is the husbandman. Every branch in me that beareth not fruit he taketh away. John 15:1-2.

Wherefore if thy hand or thy foot offend thee, cut them off, and cast them from thee: it is better for thee to enter into life halt or maimed, rather than having two hands or two feet to be cast into everlasting fire. Matthew 18:8.

This actually is an example of the mathematical concept of division in life processes. We'll discuss this, along with subtractive and multiplicative thinking, later in the book.

Without a head, the body is reduced to the random actions of a headless body. The headless body is a dysfunctional entity and, from God's perspective, an object of pity.

And should not I spare Nineveh, that <u>great city</u>, wherein are more than sixscore thousand <u>persons that cannot discern between their right hand and their left hand</u>; and <u>also</u> much cattle? Jonah 4:11.

And Jesus, when he came out, saw much people, and was moved with compassion toward them, because they were as sheep not having a shepherd: and he began to teach them many things. Mark 6:34.

Nineveh was a city of affluence in the region of modern-day Iraq. But without God's instructions to guide them, they were groping in the dark. Nineveh literally was a fat, well-fed body, flopping around, looking for its head.

God spoke through Jonah, and Nineveh found its head that day. The question is: Will we find ours? As the wise poet said, we appear fat and well-fed. And to God will not the credit give.

This must be why his power's missing: Of the rod, is not a trace.

LAST WORDS

For no man ever yet hated his own flesh; but nourisheth and cherisheth it, even as the Lord the church: For we are members of his body, of his flesh, and of his bones... This is a great mystery: but I speak concerning Christ and the church. Ephesians 5:29-32.

Look at this statement of Paul, in his letter to the Ephesians. Paul seems to be suggesting that we are body parts of Christ himself! That's sort of strange, isn't it? But Jesus said the same thing himself, in the Book of John.

I am the true vine, and my Father is the husbandman. Every branch in me that beareth not fruit he taketh away... I am the vine, ye are the branches. John 15:1-5.

Jesus Christ not only is head of his church, but he is also his <u>whole church,</u> and those that love God are his church body parts! This is a great mystery. It makes no sense if thought about logically. But spiritual observation makes mysteries disappear. And then again, no one ever accused Paul of being simple.

Hearken to me, ye that follow after righteousness, ye that seek the LORD: look unto the <u>rock whence ye are hewn</u>. Isaiah 51:1.

THE CLUB

❖

It was a beautiful sunny day, and Gillis felt relaxed as he drove down to the country club. It was a great day for several holes of golf and later, desultory conversation over a cigar and several beers.

He ruefully looked down at his pot belly. He probably should go easy on the beer. But that was a deeply ingrained club tradition. Squeeze off a few calories playing golf, gain them back—with interest—in the club lounge. He smiled dreamily as he turned right onto Kings Street. *I guess a pot belly wasn't so bad.*

He turned into the club's driveway and pulled up to the guard booth.

"What's up, Chip? You keeping them honest out here?" Chip, the grizzled old gate attendant, was in his usual spot behind the sliding-glass window. Rumor had it he'd been sitting in that same spot since before the Civil War.

"Nothing much, Bud. I do what I can." He pressed the button activating the ornamental gates and continued in his signature gravelly voice: "See ya later. Have fun in there."

Gillis "Bud" Ferguson waved as he swung the big Lincoln Navigator between the gates. "Always. See you later." His mind already was anticipating the familiar sights and smells as he drove up toward the clubhouse, a compact building framed by a tranquil backdrop of neatly manicured green lawns.

Maybe he'd beat Frank at golf this time around. He really didn't care that much about his golf handicap, though. He came here for the ambience and image.

"Hey, hey; look who's here!" Frank was edging his considerable bulk toward him at the bar. "There's some barbecue out on the deck. Come on, let's get some."

"I don't know, Frank. You know what the doctor would say."

Frank Gisborough's broad face cracked into a grin. "Yeah, yeah, he's my doc, too. Come on! Your ticker's fine!" Then, with a conspiratorial wink, "Besides, they've got those hush puppies today. Mmm, hmm."

Gillis didn't really need any further encouragement. "All right, then. Truth be told, you had me at 'barbecue.'"

The two men set out for the deck, stopping to exchange greetings and friendly camaraderie with familiar faces. After a short delay, they were on the deck, and Frank grabbed a couple of plates of heaped-up, tender pork barbecue, nestled against freshly-made hush puppies.

"Here you go." He pointed a meaty forefinger at the hush puppies on Gillis' plate. "Free fat."

Gillis looked disbelievingly at the hush puppies on his paper plate. "These are fat-free?"

"Did I say fat-free?" Frank looked around with wide-eyed innocence. "Free fat." Both men laughed as they drifted toward a group of other similarly situated men, in various stages of gustatory endeavor.

A man at the table beckoned them over with an expansive arm. "This is the life: Eat, drink, smoke, and be merry. Relax and be entertained; we've earned it."

Gillis and Frank joined the table with their munchies, exchanging verbal pleasantries, sharing jokes with a group of relaxed-looking men, one of whom went by the sobriquet "the duke."

It probably would have surprised them both to have seen the duke eight hours earlier in the club's planning committee meeting. Nine hard-nosed club executives had dispassionately worked out the direction of the club's future, including which philanthropy projects the club would be involved in over the next year, the political influence anticipated as more affluent individuals joined the club and, of course, planning the in-house entertainment.

They may have been even more surprised—and just a little offended—to hear the duke's comment about the bulk of the club members, the disparaging one about "fat cats with deep pockets needing to be entertained to keep the gravy train rolling."

Gillis and Frank didn't get to sit in on such meetings. Their job was to pay their dues and be entertained. But some may say, that's what they signed up for, wasn't it?

Their attention was captured by an ad that came on the fifty-inch plasma screen to their left. It was a short snippet of the club's financial contributions toward last month's heart week.

There were images of the club president, Joe Johnson, shaking hands with the surgeon general, smoothly fading into images with the national coordinator on dietetics for the Federal Ministry of Health, reaching a crescendo with a smiling Joe Johnson, handing over a man-sized check to the executive of the American Heart Association, to cheers and flashing cameras.

The last image was a simple black screen adorned with the club's logo and swelling music faded away to a strong, capable voice intoning the words: "The Apex Club: making a difference."

The feeling of pride, the sense of accomplishment in the lounge, was almost palpable.

"Hear, hear! It's so cool to be part of that."

"Giving back to the community; never forget where you've come from."

"That says it all, right there."

The beers got passed around, verbal commendations were swapped, food eaten, and the room became filled with the subtle aroma of plush leather mingled with food, cigars, and pipe smoke.

Gillis Ferguson, nicknamed "Bud" due to a longstanding friendship with Budweiser beers, was right in the thick of things, the memory of his two heart attacks buried in hush puppies and pork barbecue, the tangy sauce massaging away his conscience, on its way down to his belly, bathing him in a temporary aura of invincibility.

Forget your real life, your impending second divorce, your diminishing bank account and failing health; forget it all. Today you are part of something great: the Apex Club, the club of winners.

As if on cue, Joe Johnson walked into the lounge.

"There he is! There's the man!"

THE CHURCH
AS WE KNOW IT
PART I: A CHURCH LIMITED

T he power of Scripture is embodied in two commandments, which are really one: the commandment of love.

*Thou shalt love the Lord thy God with all thy heart, and
with all thy soul, and with all thy mind. This is the first
and great commandment. And the second is like unto
it, Thou shalt love thy neighbour as thyself. Matthew
22:37-38.*

This commandment reveals God's perspective for his
creation. Jesus Christ went to great lengths explaining this
perspective, in terms of its scope and implementation.

Put simply, Jesus Christ's teachings have challenged
our understanding of love by compelling us to answer three
questions.

Whom do we preach to? The audience.

What do we preach? The answer.

How do we preach? The method.

Has Christianity, as we know it today, given a more limited answer to each of these three questions than our Christian
predecessors did? The answer, unfortunately, is yes.

This chapter will flesh out how these limitations have denatured our expressions of Christianity, and why they have occurred.

The target audience of Christianity includes *everybody* or, as we recently have discovered, the church. The reason the Good Samaritan parable was given was primarily to address the question of the target audience. The scribe who triggered the telling of this parable did so by asking a question,

And who is my neighbour? Luke 10:29.

The Bible says that he wanted to justify himself. Now, there only are two reasons why an individual would choose to do this.

The first is validation by agreement. You are in agreement with a respected authority on a debated issue and want this fact known. You essentially seek validation by powering up on a skeptical audience, with an expert on the subject.

The second is validation by disagreement. You are in disagreement with another person and want to prove that individual wrong.

In both of these scenarios, you already have a committed position in the debate. This becomes a "proving" rather than a learning forum, the "See, I knew I was right!" syndrome.

The scribe had just been complimented by Jesus on being correct, regarding the importance of God's love commandment. Let's consider Jesus' answer to the scribe, and the scribe's response.

Thou hast answered right: this do, and thou shalt live. But he, willing to justify himself, said unto Jesus, And who is my neighbour? Luke 10:28-29.

If the scribe's purpose was validation by agreement, Luke 10:28 would have been a good quitting point for the discussion. He kept digging, though, looking for validation by disagreement.

What was this erudite man's problem?

He disagreed with Jesus Christ's definition of neighbor.

So, Jesus, in an allegory, defines his neighbor, whom he was supposed to love, using a Samaritan. In those days, the Samaritans and Jews were sworn enemies. Samaritans also were regarded as inferior by the Jewish people. Today, we'd call that racism.

What was Jesus Christ's take-home message?

Take a look around you. Who can we use to make this point? Let's take a group we all can agree is perceived as our worst enemy. That's right, the Samaritan. Love like the Samaritan did, as you love yourself, a Jew. Then you are fulfilling loving God with all your heart, mind, strength and soul, as the two commandments are one. Why did I choose a Samaritan to demonstrate this point? Because God made and loves the Samaritan too.

You see, if you love God, you must love who he loves. God loves all people, including you. Therefore, you must love all people, including you. However, unfortunately, many of the flag bearers of Christianity today have taken the position of the scribe.

The Samaritan is not my neighbor.

This single, seemingly harmless declaration sets the tone for future interaction with today's Samaritans.

It starts off, as did the scribe, with the wrong definition of a word. In our case, it is the word "church."

It may seem to be a trivial exercise in semantics, this insistence on proper use of the "church" word, but it obviously was important to God, since he kept finding ways to talk about it.

The extent of Satan's deception and essentially some of his most powerful tools in the earth today only can be fully appreciated by understanding the danger of redefining the boundaries of church. Why is renaming the church so dangerous?

Because it creates a surrogate goal for Christianity. The goal becomes getting people to come to church, or "churching" people. That is the first lie.

You already are in church.

You've been in it the whole time. Right from the day you were conceived in your mother's womb. But the church defined today by professed Christians has excluded essentially two thirds of the earth's populace in our lifetime, from even being a part of the church.

The sole aim for these poor, poor rejects is to become a part of "the church." If they are on the outside, they are treated the way Jesus-era Jews treated Samaritans. If they make it in, they are congratulated, high-fived, and welcomed robustly. They've been churched. They are safe.

The second lie commences once we have committed to coming to the church building. We are congratulated on the wonderful choice we have made. We are taught, as part of a general crowd, how to become a better Christ-follower. The problem is we never actually made the commitment to follow Christ.

We don't yet understand who Jesus Christ really is.

We have not been informed, fully and properly, about *who Jesus really is*.

We have not been told what to repent from, and what Jesus' title—the Word of God—really means. We don't understand that to repent and have Jesus as Lord really is a covenant of intent to follow all of God's instructions, as and when they are revealed to us, rather than follow our own imaginations. And for these reasons, we are unable to articulate who Jesus Christ really is, and what it means to follow him.

Jesus came into Galilee, preaching the <u>gospel of the kingdom of God</u>, And saying, The time is fulfilled, and the kingdom of God is at hand: <u>repent ye</u>, and believe the gospel. Mark 1:14-15.

But the <u>word of the Lord</u> endureth for ever. And <u>this is the word</u> which by the gospel is preached unto you. 1 Peter 1:25.

Now to him that is of power to stablish you according to my gospel, and the preaching of <u>Jesus Christ</u>, according to the revelation of the mystery, which was kept secret <u>since the world began</u>. Romans 16:25.

In 2005, a study by two Christian sociologists called Smith and Denton culminated in a book on teenage Christianity in America called *Soul Searching: The Religious and Spiritual Lives of American Teenagers*. Over three thousand thirteen- to seventeen-year-olds were surveyed, and two hundred and sixty-seven were interviewed directly. On direct questioning, twelve out of the two hundred and sixty-seven teens understood repentance as part of Christianity. Forty mentioned having been a sinner or understanding the concept of sinning at all. A more recent study was conducted on three thousand three hundred American teens who professed to be Christians. Professor Kenda Dean, a professor at Princeton

Theological Seminary, confirmed the same findings. Most of Dr. Dean's study group could not articulate what it meant to be Christian.

The most surprising part of both of these studies is that these teens were not only very close to their parents, but also were articulate in all other areas of social interaction. They were very sophisticated in their knowledge of the dangers of illicit drugs, celebrity trivia, sex education, etc. But on what it means to be a Christian? No dice.

These are the "church" leaders of a very quickly dawning tomorrow. They have not been properly taught by the adults, and I'm sure good, old-fashioned laziness has played a role in this sorry state of affairs. *But twelve out of two hundred and sixty-seven?* That is less than four and a half percent!

Is it possible, just possible, that the professed Christian adults cannot teach their children because they really don't know themselves? Obviously, you can't give what you don't have. But I'm being diplomatic. Jesus put it a little bit more starkly.

Let them alone: they be blind leaders of the blind. And if the blind lead the blind, both shall fall into the ditch. Matthew 15:14.

So, we are now in the building called church, learning the Bible stories and the Bible lingo about Abraham, Peter, Moses, and Jesus. We read about one astounding miracle after the other. But then, in the not so distant future, the third lie is revealed. Suddenly people start to call you a Christian, or one of the "saints."

There's only one problem. You have learned that Jesus Christ is the same, yesterday, today, and forever; you even can quote the location of that Bible verse, Hebrews 13:8. But where are those astounding Jesus miracles today? Maybe other church members have miracle stories you can learn from, or the pastor will give real life examples? Is that not what the Bible says to do?

> *Now is come salvation, and strength, and the kingdom of our God, and the <u>power of his Christ</u>: for the accuser of our brethren is cast down, which accused them before our God day and night. And they overcame him by the blood of the Lamb, and by <u>the word of their testimony</u>. Revelation 12:11.*

> *But to do good and to <u>communicate</u> forget not: for with such sacrifices God is <u>well pleased</u>. Hebrews 13:16.*

But it is impolite to ask, and no one's talking. Besides, you might sound foolish for asking. Especially now, with everyone calling you Christian Brother, Sister, and Saint, and all. After a while, you start to believe them.

And what of those biblical miracles, those miracles you could learn and benefit from? Hebrews 13:8 takes on a subtle nuance. "Of course Jesus is the same today as he was yesterday! But Bible miracles don't happen as dramatically today as they did back then. I'm just not recognizing the miracles of today," you opine. So, you redefine "miracle" to mean getting a good parking spot, during rush hour, at work.

Forget that you fully recognized and understood the Bible miracles in all of their jaw-dropping splendor when you read them. Forget that jaw-dropping miracles are as much a part of the Christian journey as feet are to walking, and that without one, you legitimately have to question the presence of the other. Forget what Jesus Christ said, in the Gospel of John.

> *Verily, verily, I say unto you, He that believeth on me, <u>the works that I do shall he do also</u>; and <u>greater works</u> than these shall he do; because I go unto my Father. John 14:12.*

That would be too much to expect. And so we diminish our Christianity to suit our societal experience, and a false doctrine—a powerless version of Christianity—is born. It is a false doctrine that gives wings to other viewpoints that say biblical miracles are just metaphors, and did not literally occur as they were written.

This is a legitimate challenge, stemming from the powerless Christianity we have created. The Bible's presentation never would be in question if we were doing what Christ said and did. But what is our response? Bull-headed anger at their effrontery.

The unfortunate truth is that the atheist or "free thinker" only attacks the house we've built. It's not their fault you built your house on a flimsy foundation.

You have tried to build a Christian house on a non-Christian foundation.

That foundation is supposed to be made of rock. But your house is built on sand. And deep down in your soul, you know it, too, even if you don't admit it. Jesus is the foundation upon which your Christian house is built. And you never really accepted him.

Whosoever cometh to me, and heareth my sayings, and doeth them, I will shew you to whom he is like: He is like a man which built an house, and digged deep, and laid the foundation on a rock. Luke 6:47-48.

And did all drink the same spiritual drink: for they drank of that spiritual Rock that followed them: and that Rock was Christ. 1 Corinthians 10:4.

And what about the Great Commission? Do people still even use that phrase? I think I've heard it used less than a handful of times this century. This is the part about actually preaching the gospel of God. When was the last time you talked to someone about repentance, about doing the instructions of Christ for a better life in this world, and the one to come? When was the last time someone actually repented right in front of you, *because of you?*

And he said unto them, Go ye into all the world, and <u>preach the gospel</u> to every creature. Mark 16:15.

For though I preach the gospel, I have nothing to glory of: for <u>necessity is laid upon me</u>; yea, woe is unto me, if I preach not the gospel! 1 Corinthians 9:16.

Do you see what Paul said? Preaching the gospel is a *necessity.* But we are still confused about our own doctrine. Once again, we can't give what we don't have. Besides, it might be intrusive to engage people on those terms. So we hold our peace.

But the vacuum of unfinished business remains—the vacuum left by incomplete doctrine and the lack of truly remarkable stories to share. Nature hates vacuums and will fill them, every chance it gets.

And so, let the fun and games begin. Usher in the church activities, and fund drives, and entertainment. They're not intrinsically bad activities in themselves. But these usually good activities fill a void that they were never meant to fill. The void that is a *lack of proper doctrine, spiritual fruits, and miraculous works.*

Every branch in me that beareth not fruit he taketh away: and every <u>branch</u> that beareth fruit, he purgeth it, that it may bring forth more fruit. John 15:2.

Even so faith, if it hath not works, is <u>dead</u>, being alone. Yea, a man may say, Thou hast faith, and I have works:

shew me thy faith without thy works, and I will shew thee my faith by my works. James 2:17-18.

Miracles are replaced by church activities. Love and goodness are replaced by entertainment and church social events. Pleasant activities that make you feel good and happy, especially when you are in the church building, which you spend more and more time in because, in the building, you feel better.

In that 2005 teenage study, being happy—or references to it in the context of the church—was mentioned by one hundred and twelve teenagers, more than two thousand times. They obviously were happy in the church building, but just didn't understand what they were doing there.

But "happy days" have nothing to do with life outside the "church," which we desperately try to forget, because it is no better than when we were "unchurched." God's magnificent vision of the church somehow has been changed by the sons and daughters of men into a *club*.

We have changed church into a privileged club membership.

As with all clubs, you have a handful of people in executive positions, in charge of the deep machinations of the club, such as collection of dues to fund and organize diversionary entertainment for other club members—other club members, if I may point out, who are in the vast majority and do essentially nothing.

Once I'm in the club, I'm safe.

Unfortunately, the hollowness of the club's position of "safety" is especially noticed by people of a non-Christian background who have joined a church denomination in search of a deeper meaning to life.

This phenomenon is borne out by the atheist movement in the world today. A study carried out in 2004 showed that in the 1990s, there was a large bump in conversion from *compulsory* atheism to Christianity.

This corresponded to the dissolution of the Soviet Bloc, where atheism was state law rather than a choice. However, even preceding this, there has been a steady increase in *voluntary atheism* worldwide, especially in America.

Sixteen percent of youth between the ages of fifteen and twenty-five do not believe in God as a supreme deity, as opposed to nine percent in 1993. Adults showed a similar— though slower—trend. The attrition to atheism appears to be mainly from Protestant Christian populations.

What is going on here? The compulsory atheist is convinced to become a Christian, while the Christian, *the insider*, steps out to become an atheist? The key to understanding this trend rests in subsequent events, once we cross the threshold of joining a church denomination.

The would-be Christian convert comes in the doorway to what he hopes are the unimaginable wonders of God's kingdom. And then, nothing. The scholar who came seeking life tools but got entertainment instead is left thinking: *Is this what all the hoopla was about?*

Some stay in the "church" setup, waiting for something better before they jump ship. Others sit back and embrace the deceptively seductive, almost narcotic tug to be passive, and change nothing.

Other individuals step out of the hypocrisy, usually back to where they came from. After all, some may say, better the devil you know than the one you don't—at least until a saint comes along. But hope becomes bitter disillusionment.

It almost feels as if the saints don't live here anymore.

LAST WORDS

It almost feels as if the saints don't live here anymore.
A lot of outsiders who have tried to embrace the hope that
is Christianity have held this viewpoint. But what about
the insider, the professed Christian who has lived around
Christianity their whole life?

Unfortunately the insider's pattern is more often than
not to patent Christianity. God is treated like a pharmaceu-
tical drug with different trade names, marketed by pundits
competing against each other. The insider creates God, in his
own image. Never mind if God sees it differently.

God created man in his own image. Genesis 1:27.

The outsider is disillusioned, but the insider, he's a different animal. He's a *snob,* who is largely unaware of how
snobbish he really is. He believes the saints are alive and
well, which would be very good except for one little detail.
The insider's particular brand of drug is better. And all the
saints now live in his house.

THE SNOB

J une Ballantyne was a snob.
Her nickname was the "Ice Queen" to her detractors, and they were many. Her long nose was always disdainfully turned upwards, as if to ward off a bad smell. She had perfected the subtle art of skewering you to the wall with one contemptous glance. Even her name sounded snooty. Yeah, it was official. She was the neighborhood snob.

The only thing she lacked to complete the icy picture was a scandalously expensive home, huge yard, and a fancy car—the actual *financial creds* to back the image up. I guess God had been merciful to the rest of us.

But there was mutiny afoot in the Ballantyne neighborhood. She may have the most haughty manner and though everyone hated to admit it, make the best peach cobbler this side of the Mississippi River, but all her neighbors by mutual consent had decided she would *not* have the most neatly manicured lawn.

So, the homes that surrounded the "Ballantyne homestead" made a pact. After all, the enemy of my enemy is my friend. They mowed their lawns so frequently that Miss June's grass had no choice but to look bushy by comparison.

They phoned each other with glee as they watched poor Mr. Ballantyne unsuccessfully trying to keep up with the new neighborhood standard. He seemed nice enough, but if he'd *married* the woman, he must have some bad in him.

All spring long the lawnmower wars raged. Then one day in early summer Jeannie peeked out of her customary "spy" window and saw an ambulance in the Ballantyne front yard. A frail-looking Mr. Ballantyne was being loaded into the back of the ambulance.

All animosity forgotten for a moment, she stepped out onto her front porch and walked across to the Ballantyne yard, just as the ambulance sped off.

"Miss June? What's going on?"

June Ballantyne was standing ramrod straight in the middle of her front yard, staring after the receding ambulance. She turned.

"Joe collapsed after mowing the lawn. They think it is probably heat exhaustion or a stroke; he's not as young as he used to be. I... I've got to get to the hospital."

Jeannie felt a sharp stab of guilt.

"Oh I'm so sorry! I'll drive you there. I'll just get my truck."

She trotted briskly across to her yard, jumped in her ancient Ford pickup truck and drove over to the front of the Ballantyne home, beckoning June over. The Ice Queen hesitated, and seemingly out of nowhere, Jeannie felt animosity flare.

"Look, today I'm driving you to the hospital. You can turn your nose up at my truck tomorrow." With that she threw open the passenger door.

"Get in."

Mrs. Ballantyne got in.

As Jeannie drove the old banger into the afternoon traffic, she couldn't help but notice her passenger's disapproving glance at her jalopy's worn out, not very clean interior. That was the last straw.

"Why are you such a snob?"

June looked over, in surprise.

"Me a snob? I just act lady-like! That's how I was raised. All of your lawn mowing and carrying on has almost put my poor Joseph in the grave, what with him trying to keep up. You're a fine one to talk!"

Jeannie's guilt swelled, but she blustered,

"I don't know what you're talking about."

The arctic gaze. "Yes you do. You're a lawn mowing snob."

"*Me*? A snob? That's the most ridiculous thing I've ever heard!"

But June Ballantyne had made her point. With all the dignity she could muster she settled back in her seat. Jeannie never stood a chance.

Later, as they sat side by side in the hospital's waiting area, the Ice Queen gave Jeannie a funny look.

"From one snob to another, thank you. I will never forget your friendship today."

Jeannie, slightly mollified, couldn't resist a quick retort.

"About time!" And then, more wryly, in an implied admission of guilt,

"With enemies like me, what are friends for? You're welcome."

Was that a truce? Today, possibly. Tomorrow? I wouldn't bet on it.

THE CHURCH
AS WE KNOW IT
PART II: PRIDE'S FOLLY

S o, there you have it. A church redefined, a savior dimin-
ished, and a way of living denatured to cater to personal
tastes and pleasure. We have created a poor facsimile of the
real thing. But it isn't as if we weren't warned about this.
Let's listen in on Paul, in his letter to Timothy.

> *This know also, that in the last days perilous times shall*
> *come. For men shall be lovers of their own selves...*
> *lovers of pleasures more than lovers of God; Having a*
> *form of godliness, but denying the power thereof: from*
> *such turn away. 2 Timothy 3:2-5.*

But how did we get in this mess, redefining church in
the first place? The answer is simple, but not easy. In fact,
I dedicated a whole chapter to this polarizing phenomenon,
earlier on in this book: *Competition.*

It puts asunder what God has put together: in this case,
his church. It's the same old book, just a different chapter.

That great splitter called Satan climbed into the head of
a young man called Cain years ago, and by perverting com-

petition, made him kill his own brother. The devil has been hanging out in mankind's head ever since.

It was he who suggested to someone many years ago, before either you or I were born, to tag on a few words, a little alphabet soup, to describe our church, based on something other than its location.

The only qualification God has put to the word "church" in Scripture is based on its *physical location.* The seven churches in the Book of Revelation are divided on the basis of location in the Asia Minor of the First Century, in the ancient cities of Sardis, Philadelphia, etc. Paul's letters are to the church in different *locations:* Ephesians to those at the city of Ephesus, Romans to those at the place called Rome, etc.

This is much the same as having a chain of department stores in different locations. The store's name may stay as Macy's, no matter the location. The same goods are sold in both stores according to—hopefully—the same standards.

Salute the brethren which are in Laodicea, and Nymphas, and the church which is in his house. And when this epistle is read among you, cause that it be read also in the church of the Laodiceans; and that ye likewise read the epistle from Laodicea. Colossians 4:15-16.

They still are really one church, with one doctrine.

Then came the paradigm shift. A church decided to name itself based on who they perceived themselves to be: a superior people. The first of the really big ones is The Roman Catholic Church.

Unlike Paul's "Romans" letter which was location-based, this Roman Catholic Church was based on the people's perception of who they were. And it has gone downhill ever since. After this came the Lutheran Church, named after *one man*: Martin Luther. Then came John Calvin's Calvinists, the Methodists, the Presbyterians, the Anglicans, and so on. How come we never see in the Bible the Peterist, Paulan, or Johnist church? Those wise men knew better than to add their names to the name God had given. God has very specific reasons for defining church the way he did. It is primarily done for simplicity, clarity, and to eliminate snobbery. However, people are consumed with the "mine is better than yours" syndrome. Like June Ballantyne and "Jeannie,"

We have walked around with an elitist mentality.

Oh, we like to call it smarts, maturity, privilege, and exclusivity, but as discussed in the earlier chapter that bears its name, competition when misdirected becomes just a good, old-fashioned birthplace for pride and lies, aimed at keeping up appearances.

Unfortunately, God hates both attitudes with a passion. I don't know too much about the workings of the universe, but one thing I do know: We really don't want to get God upset.

These six things doth the LORD hate: yea, seven are an abomination unto him: A proud look, a lying tongue, and hands that shed innocent blood. Proverbs 6:16-17.

It may seem to be a trivial exercise in semantics, this insistence on proper use of the "church" word, but it was obviously important to God, since He keeps finding ways to talk about it!

If God says the definition of "church" is important, then it is crucial that we take the same position. And if we think it is just a simple question of semantics, let us remember a little descriptive term that has caused a maelstrom for four hundred years: Negro. It means the color black in Spanish. Pretty harmless, right?

The scope of God's perspective has been narrowed down to what has been imagined to be God's elite club, "the church" or the "true Christians," much like the "true sons of Abraham," or the Jews, in Jesus' day.

They answered and said unto him, Abraham is our father. Jesus saith unto them, If ye were Abraham's children, ye would do the works of Abraham. John 8:39.

This "true Christians" concept has been practiced by the Baptists, the Church of Christ, Assemblies of God, Seventh-day Adventists, interdenominational churches and even, despite the rhetoric of reform, the Roman Catholic Church.

"Pope Benedict XVI has reasserted the universal primacy of the Roman Catholic Church, approving a document released Tuesday that says Orthodox churches were defective and that other Christian denominations were not true churches.—Nicole Winfield, the Associated Press, July 10, 2007.

The Pope's secret password to God's bedside telephone lies in the word "Catholic," I guess.

This is not how God sees us and *not* what Jesus taught! God gave us the scope of his commandment so that our minds can perceive mankind as he does. Understanding the full boundaries of church flays away the exclusivity clause, showing clearly that church is not created by *some* men and women, but is the default position of *all* men and women, to a functional purpose.

If you do not fulfill your place within this ultimate purpose, you are non-functioning, or dysfunctional. The aim of the gospel of the kingdom of God, therefore, is to provide tools for the church to function correctly, rather than to join a sect called "church," by whatever shifting sand definition we choose to call it.

A chameleon church can be redefined according to an individual's wishes, at will, depending on the prevailing circumstance. Such a church is driven by man's will from its very definition, rather than God's.

To this end, some have made the club even more exclusive: Only those who speak in tongues, perhaps, are the true enlightened Christians; hence, true neighborly behavior is extended only to fellow club members. A polite smile and a quick crossing of the road is reserved for non-members, the Samaritans. Sound familiar?

Always remember that attitude springs from perception.

Jesus Christ died for the dysfunctional church, to make it functional.

LAST WORDS

Dividing church up into clubs as we have done makes us run them as all worldly clubs are typically run: with a strong dollop of politics and self interest. This is not a new concept. The prophet Jonah did not want to preach to the people in Nineveh, a large Assyrian city located in the area of modern-day Iraq, whose affluence and influence was a threat to the Hebrew people.

But it displeased Jonah exceedingly, and he was very angry. And he prayed unto the LORD, and said, I pray thee, O LORD, was not this my saying, when I was yet in my country?... I knew that thou art a gracious God, and merciful, slow to anger, and of great kindness, and repentest thee of the evil. Jonah 4:1-2.

Jonah would rather have seen the Ninevites burn, eliminating the competition permanently. But God was determined to save Nineveh, because *God loved the Assyrians too.*

And should not I spare Nineveh, that great city, wherein are more than sixscore thousand persons that cannot discern between their right hand and their left hand; and also much cattle? Jonah 4:11.

God is love, Jonah is political, and from where I stand, we've been modern-day Jonahs. Oh, but now we are delving into matters for the next chapter: the separation of church and state. Let's not get ahead of ourselves, now.

THE ELECTION

✤

"Is there any such thing as a successful politician with integrity? Come on now, let's be real. Power corrupts." The year was 2006, and the topic of discussion was the recent election in Kolyastan, the run-off election between the incumbent premier and the vigorous young farmer from an opposition party. It was a sham of a democratic process, as everyone knew that there was really only one candidate running: the premier himself.

The world watched with interest, and the media focused on this tiny country of less than one million as the election drama unfolded.

It had all the ingredients of a diabolical soap opera: an old, corrupt dictator; a young visionary with a groundswell of support but no political clout; a highly visible statesman whose political bubble was burst by a strategically exposed illicit love affair; and a shocking poisoning of the only female candidate running.

Suddenly four candidates had been slashed to two, and the world rooted for the underdog—all the while "knowing" he didn't have a hope of winning. Of course, the whole unfolding drama was prime fodder for discussion, even in church small groups.

"Look at what is happening in Kolyastan: Batchi... Batchiav... whatever his name is, he has been sitting in that seat oppressing the people for years. God is watching."

"Yes, but the young farmer cannot win. The old establishment is too deeply entrenched."

"That's right. The corruption runs too deep. You know Kolyastan is the world's third largest center for human trafficking?"

Several horrified gasps.

"How awful!"

"Oh, the poor lost souls."

"I didn't know that. Where did you hear that?"

"They showed it as a special on Fox."

"That's the kind of thing this country should step up and fight against. That is just wrong."

"But what are we going to fight with? All our troops are tied up in Iraq and Afghanistan. Besides, it is written that these things will happen in the end times. Father will turn against son, daughter against mother, iniquity will abound."

"That's right. We have to stand firm on God's word and the gospel to the end. Is the farmer a Christian?"

No one seemed to know for sure.

"I am guessing he is not, or we would have heard of his faith by now."

"Maybe he has a private faith."

"That's a shame. Wouldn't this be a good time to have God on his side, for God to show up with a miracle? As we know from Scripture, with God everything is possible."

A spattering of emphatic amens around the group.

"At least, they have started on the path to freedom and democracy. They have come a long way."

"Yes, freedom. Whatever else one may say about this country, God has blessed us so much, with democracy and freedom."

"You got that right. The Republicans may not always get it right, but at least they respect God and Jesus. As for Al Gore and all that popular vote business, if Al Gore, with all his global warming talk was to have won the election, this country would have gone straight down the tubes."

"Yeah, but the Republicans have messed up, too. Look at the FEMA-Katrina fiasco."

"Agreed, they have been a disappointment. They're much better than the Democrats, though. They believe in Jesus."

"All that tree-hugging, animal-loving posturing of the Democrats is just to get elected. Global warming, PETA, all that stuff is not important. What we need is Jesus."

A chorus of affirmative nods.

"Amen!"

"At least here, no one's getting poisoned!"

"Amen, brother! If Jesus were here today, I bet he would be a Republican."

Laughs all around. "How did we get off on this topic anyway? Let's get started. On Sunday, Pastor shared with us 1 Peter..."

THE SEPARATION OF CHURCH AND STATE
PART I: THE NAKED TRUTH

⛭

W hat is this business about merging Christianity with political ideology? Jesus, a *Republican?* I think someone misread their Scripture. I seem to recall Jesus hanging out with *publicans*, not Republicans.

Humor aside, I have heard this opinion voiced *more than once* by professed Christians. So, maybe this isn't such harmless humor, after all.

The living church is not supposed to be lumped together with a political party. One cannot, with parity, compare these two entities. It is like comparing God and man. The greater entity is supposed to positively influence the activities of the lesser, if the latter so chooses.

> *For as the heavens are higher than the earth, so are my ways higher than your ways, and my thoughts than your thoughts. Isaiah 55:9.*

Political entities look for the best possible solutions available to deal with people's problems. It is the job of the living church to showcase effective solutions to these very problems. If we, the living church, are doing our work correctly, we don't need to ring a bell along the halls of Congress to be heard, or sneak carrier pigeons to politicians, entreating them to do the work for us. Policy makers will seek the church out for advice. They did so with Jesus. They will do so with you.

And there were certain Greeks among them that came up to worship at the feast: The same came therefore to Philip, which was of Bethsaida of Galilee, and desired him, saying, Sir, we would see Jesus. Philip cometh and telleth Andrew: and again Andrew and Philip tell Jesus. John 12:20-22.

A less humorous issue than heavenly partisanship is the commonly held concept that a Christian's freedom is the same as personal freedom. Where on earth did we get this idea? Certainly not from Jesus!

For he that is called in the Lord, being a servant, is the Lord's freeman: likewise also he that is called, being free, is Christ's servant. 1 Corinthians 7:22.

Freedom or servitude as the world defines it has absolutely no relevance to freedom from God's point of view. Our worldly idea of freedom is based on the state of our *souls*. Jesus freedom is based on the state of our *spirits*.

That which is born of the flesh is flesh; and that which is born of the Spirit is spirit. John 3:6.

Verily, verily, I say unto thee, Except a man be born of water and of the Spirit, he cannot enter into the kingdom of God. John 3:5.

Personal freedoms—such as freedom of speech, gun usage, or the freedom to publicly attend a church building—come by due democratic process in politics and government; they are *freedoms of the soul*. Spiritual freedom enables you to do God's will unfettered by personal circumstances.

I have learned, in whatsoever state I am, therewith to be content. I know both how to be abased, and I know how to abound: every where and in all things I am instructed both to be full and to be hungry, both to abound and to suffer need. I can do all things through Christ which strengtheneth me. Philippians 4:11-13.

Jesus actually advocated *capturing souls!* This is the same thing as capturing *the minds of men*. Remember those boring definitions on mind, soul, and spirit at the beginning of the book? This is where they really come in handy!

And Jesus said unto them, Come ye after me, and I will make you to become fishers of men. Mark 1:17.

Casting down imaginations, and every high thing that exalteth itself against the knowledge of God, and bringing into captivity every thought to the obedience of Christ. 2 Corinthians 10:5.

Your freedom in God, therefore, has nothing to do with your country's current state of freedom or servitude. If you make them one and the same, your allegiance to God wavers between God and country. You have created a double-minded individual. It does not pay to mingle church and state.

For he that wavereth is like a wave of the sea driven with the wind and tossed. For let not that man think that he shall receive any thing of the Lord. A double minded man is unstable in all his ways. James 1:6-8.

The strange thing is, even if we use personal freedoms in a worldly sort of way, are we really as free as we think?

Our way of life has debt deeply ingrained as a societal norm. It masquerades as credit card debt, mortgage debt, bank loan debt, car payments, or whatever we choose to call it. It has been classified as good debt, bad debt, educational debt. Individual debt is expected and proudly sold as a desirable commodity in this society. Is this the freedom we aim to keep?

The rich ruleth over the poor, and the borrower is servant to the lender. Proverbs 22:7.

Our culture and tradition has people getting fatter and sicker each year, based on poor dietary choices and a sedentary lifestyle. Obesity reigns, arthritis pains, and we stagger along with an insatiable sweet tooth that turns laughter to sorrow as we succumb to disease, huge hospital bills, and inevitable financial ruin. This is the culture we so "freely" choose to preserve?

He that loveth pleasure shall be a poor man. Proverbs 21:17.

For the drunkard and the glutton shall come to poverty. Proverbs 23:21.

But she that liveth in pleasure is dead while she liveth. 1 Timothy 5:6.

Tied to this idea of personal freedom is a perception of wealth, a presumption of affluence, birthed by an abundance of creature comforts and conveniences. But how rich are we really?

By current estimates, the U.S. has the largest debt of any country in the world, a whopping thirteen trillion dollars. Of this amount, more than four trillion dollars officially is recognized as the amount owed to other countries. At the top of that list of foreign owners comes The People's Republic of China, the country we love to hate, with over one trillion dollars, closely followed by Japan, who we used to hate.

Believe it or not, the U.S. owes *Russia* one hundred and fifty-one billion dollars, and owes Venezuela big money. In fact, the U.S. has owed money in all the years of its existence as a country except for one year: 1835, under the presidency of President Andrew Jackson of Tennessee.

So, unless you were born in 1835, you are not born free, even if Kid Rock thinks you are. And unless you have paid your share of this nation's debt, all forty-three thousand dollars of it at the last count, you are not rich, even if you passed the Dave Ramsey course for a debt-free existence.

How many of you remember the old tale of the Emperor's new clothes?

The emperor was told he had on the most beautiful attire and believed it, strolling proudly through the streets of his empire *naked* because he had been deceived, privately laughed at by his subjects until a little child, with some graphic pointing, let him in on the cruel joke.

People have been deceived into believing we are sitting in the lap of luxury, riches, and a special favor of "creature comforts," bestowed from on high. "God has blessed America, above all other nations in the world," we say.

Well there is another perspective on our current circumstances: a sobering, naked truth. I'm sorry, but living the good life on somebody else's dollar does not a rich man make.

Because thou sayest, I am rich, and increased with goods, and have need of nothing; and knowest not that thou art wretched, and miserable, and poor, and blind, and naked. Revelation 3:17.

It creates a naked emperor.

LAST WORDS

How do you view debt? For most of us, debt is our very own personal red-headed stepchild, the embarrassing relative we'd love to forget. However, for most of us, the current economic climate has made it painfully clear that debt is very much part of the family. He sits, boldly making decisions, in Daddy's seat at the kitchen table.

Him that speaketh from heaven: Whose voice then shook the earth: but now he hath promised, saying, Yet once more I shake not the earth only, but also heaven. Hebrews 12:25-26.

So, the circumstances created by God's shaking have made us own up—albeit reluctantly—to our personal debt. But what about the national debt? Who owes that money?

We do.

THE SMALL,
POWERFUL MAN

О nce upon a time, there was a small but powerful man who went to war for the good of mankind.

After several years of heroic fighting, the strong little fellow won his war. However, he had invested all he had to fight this war. The little strong man was broke. So he went, cap in hand, for a loan from his big friend, a friend who had helped him win the war. The little strong man got his loan, and started to repair his house.

About ten years later, a troublemaker tried to take over the little strong man's vacation home, because it had a great view of the Mediterranean Sea. The little powerhouse, supported by a business associate that lived down the street from him, recaptured his vacation home with a view. But he did not tell his big friend about his vacation home troubles.

When his big friend learned of the small powerful man's vacation home exploits, he got very angry. He felt he had a right to know, since the little strong man was using his money. The big friend felt it was rash and risky, and could have caused another expensive war against mankind. And all over a vacation home? He decided to teach the little strong man a lesson.

So the big friend asked the little strong man to move out of his Mediterranean vacation home. If the powerful little fellow didn't, he was going to have to pay back the money he owed, or go to jail.

The little strong man weighed his options. Glumly, he saw that none of them were good. Humiliated, the little strong man moved out of his vacation home with a view. It became quite clear that he was just a little man now. Samson's hair was shorn, and his power was gone.

Living in relative obscurity, it took him more than fifty years to pay off his loan. Actually, he just paid it off in 2006.

THE SEPARATION OF CHURCH AND STATE
PART II: THE ROAD TO JOBLESSNESS AND THE LOSS OF MORAL INFLUENCE

⚜

It is good to learn the lessons of history. The little strong man was Great Britain under Prime Minister Anthony Eden; his big friend was the U.S. under President Dwight D. Eisenhower. The business associate was France and the troublemaker, Egypt. The year was 1956, and the vacation home with a view was the Suez Canal.

So, Great Britain, installment by installment, paid three and a half billion dollars to the U.S. up until 2006, when the debt was paid in full. The British currently do not owe the U.S. any of that debt money at all. But who is the Number Three foreign country that the U.S. owes? This one surprised even me: Great Britain. More than two hundred and seventy-two billion dollars, to be exact. This is more than the U.S. owes all of the oil exporting nations combined.

It looks like Samson has regrown his hair. I'd watch out, if I were you.

So, getting back to that question: "What does it matter how much we owe? What does this story have to do with me?" The simple one word answer for you is: *jobs*.

The jobs go where the money is. It's that simple. The lender gets to dictate terms. So the terms of those loans from China, Japan, Saudi Arabia, and all those countries we love to hate dictate where the jobs and infrastructure for those jobs go — primarily to their people, both in their country, and yours.

The stranger that <u>is</u> within thee shall get up above thee very high; and thou shalt come down very low. He shall lend to thee, and thou shalt not lend to him: he shall be the head, and thou shalt be the tail. Deuteronomy 28:43-44.

So, Toyota, primarily a Japanese company that makes great cars, can have a factory in Georgetown, Kentucky, on a 1500 acre plot of land given to this company for free. So, you have economic recovery, but no jobs in your country.

God told you: The borrower *is servant to the lender.*

But we are blind to these painful truths. Such blindness is the result of going down a road of logical, rather than spiritual, Christianity.

Before I wrap this up, I am compelled to discuss one more area of distorted biblical truth that has arisen from the seamless mingling of church and state. This area has led to repercussions that have reverberated through the length and breadth of the professed American living church. This is in the uncomfortable area of taxes.

No one likes taxes, except probably the tax collector, and that's only because it's his job. He certainly doesn't enjoy paying taxes when his own tax day rolls around. But should the living church pay taxes?

As you have probably figured out by now, I'm one of those literal Bible-thumping individuals. I really believe that the solutions to life's problems lie within the pages of the Holy Book itself, if only we would take the time to look for them.

I'm not a "What would Jesus do?" kind of guy. I'm a "What has Jesus done?" sort of fellow. So, I'm going to look up "Jesus" and "taxes" in the Great Book, and see what he has to say on the matter. Just as one would have it, there's a nice tax story in Matthew 17.

And when they were come to Capernaum, they that received tribute money came to Peter, and said, Doth not your master pay tribute? He saith, <u>Yes</u>. Matthew 17:24-25.

So far, it looks as if Jesus paid the "tribute." Tribute is actually the old English word for taxes; open and shut case. At least Peter seemed to think so, and he would know Jesus' tax-paying habits, given that he hung out with the man himself for three years.

But the story gets better, because we get to see Jesus' reaction to the tax query when Peter walks into the house.

And when he was come into the house, Jesus prevented him, saying, What thinkest thou, Simon? of whom do the kings of the earth take custom or tribute? of their own children, or of strangers? Peter saith unto him, Of strangers. Matthew 17:25-26.

Children who own the kingdom should not be taxed on what is theirs already. Strangers pay taxes—or "tribute"—for the privilege of being in the kingdom. Children maintain the smooth running of the kingdom. So, it appears that Jesus thought free sons of Israel, of whom he counted himself one, ideally should not pay taxes.

But what did Jesus *do?* That was the whole point of this exercise, wasn't it?

Jesus saith unto him, Then are the children free. Notwithstanding, <u>lest we should offend them</u>, go thou to the sea, and cast an hook, and take up the fish that first cometh up; and when thou hast opened his mouth, thou shalt find a piece of money: that take, and give unto them for me and thee. Matthew 17:26-27.

Love should always shape the way we think.

Jesus showed the law of *love,* a law that superseded the law of a son's rights within a kingdom. Rather than offend them and give them cause to resent him and not follow his teachings, Jesus paid the taxes, using the opportunity to squeeze off a private miracle for Peter in the process.

Jesus paid the taxes.

In 1954, legislation was passed spearheaded by then-Senator, later to become President Lyndon B. Johnson, listing churches as tax-exempt entities. This legislation created what is known as 501(c)(3) tax-exempt status for churches and all charitable organizations in the U.S.A. This seemingly good deal comes at a price.

Under the Internal Revenue Code, all section 501(c) (3) organizations are absolutely prohibited from directly or indirectly participating in, or intervening in, any political campaign on behalf of (or in opposition to) any candidate for elective public office...

Violating this prohibition may result in denial or revocation of tax-exempt status and the imposition of certain excise taxes…voter education or registration activities with evidence of bias that (a) would favor one candidate over another; (b) oppose a candidate in some manner; or (c) have the effect of favoring a candidate or group of candidates, will constitute prohibited participation or intervention.

Senator Lyndon B. Johnson did not want to hear what "charitably exempted entities" had to say about American society, and the way the country was governed, from the seats of political influence in Washington. The 501(c)(3) is nothing more than a legislated gag order.

He wanted to shut them up.

You see, we never did ask why the ancient Jewish version of the Internal Revenue Service approached Jesus for taxes in the first place. He wasn't the only man in Israel. Why didn't they ask Peter for his taxes? We know Peter hadn't paid them, as the money in the fish's mouth was for both Jesus and Peter. Why Jesus?

They wanted to shut him up.

His mission was on a collision course with theirs, so they were getting ready to whip up public sentiment that he was a money-hungry hypocrite possessed of a silver tongue. Jesus understood all that, and paid his taxes.

I am yet to find a church that has refused the 501(c)(3) tax exempt provision here in the U.S.

So, the professed American church lives under a ball and chain. Whenever Satan wants to forward his purposes in America, he drags the moral topics of his interest out of our homes, schools, and local workplaces, and drops them into the political arena.

For more than fifty years, the ones who were the designated moral lamps of their society have sat down in a corner and moped, selling off their right to free speech, for a few lousy dollars. The people who have called themselves churches are steadily losing their ability to positively impact society, and they don't know why.

I'm here to tell you why: you sold your birthright away for a bowl of soup more than fifty years ago! If you are going to follow Jesus, follow him, and stop just pretending to do so! Anything less and you are good for nothing else, but to be trampled underfoot by the sons and daughters of men.

Ye are the salt of the earth: but if the salt has lost his savour, wherewith shall it be salted? it is thenceforth good for nothing, but to be cast out, and to be trodden under foot of men. Matthew 5:13.

So, given what you now know, what do you think? I think there should definitely be a separation of church and state, *from the church's viewpoint*. Give unto Caesar what is Caesar's, and unto God what is God's. And as for the state?

What the state does is up to them.

THE SEPARATION OF CHURCH AND STATE
DEEPER THOUGHTS

☩

Paul once asked the question in Galatians 4:16: "Am I therefore become your enemy, because I tell you the truth?" Now, remember: Just because it is true does not mean we have to like it. I do not enjoy the truths I have just told.

But I don't get to ignore the passages of Scripture that don't suit me. I refuse to knowingly deceive myself, no matter how tempting it is to do so. Therefore, I refuse to evenly mingle church and state. I refuse to make democracy indistinguishable from God. I refuse to make Democrats the devil. And I refuse to make Jesus a Republican.

The truth hurts like the dickens, but in this case, hurt is the beginning of restoration. I hope we can turn away from the destructive way of thinking that is ripping apart the very fabric of this land. But to do so, we have to see ourselves as we really are, *before* we can be transformed into who we were meant to be.

Jacob, the son of the Bible patriarch Isaac, was an ambitious trickster. His very name means "the supplanter," and Jacob lived up to his name, fighting *in the womb* to be born first and ahead of his twin brother Esau.

And Isaac intreated the LORD for his wife...and Rebekah his wife conceived. And the children struggled together within her... there were twins in her womb... And the first came out... after that came his brother out... and his name was called Jacob. Genesis 25:21-26.

He lost that birthday battle, but he continued fighting, using artifice to get ahead through trickery. He never owned up to his name, choosing to present himself as someone he wasn't, humble and meek when he actually was fiercely driven and ambitious. He stole his brother's blessing and tricked his father-in-law Laban, becoming wealthy at the latter's expense.

But when the cattle were feeble, he put them not in: so the feebler were Laban's, and the stronger Jacob's. Genesis 30:42.

And Jacob said unto his father, I am Esau thy firstborn. Genesis 27:19.

And when Esau heard the words of his father, he cried... Is not he rightly named Jacob? for he hath supplanted me these two times: he took away my birthright; and behold, now he hath taken away my blessing. Genesis 27:34-36.

He played the game well and answered to anything but his name, until an angel showed up one day. After wrestling all night with this angelic being, an injured Jacob—in his typical "seize the moment" fashion—insisted on being blessed by his formidable adversary. And then a strange thing happened: The angel asked him one simple question.

What is thy name?

Suddenly, there it was. After an exhausting night of trying to win another fight with his own strength, cunning, and rudimentary wrestling skills—the angel put Jacob's hip socket out with just one touch—Jacob finally understood his problem: He was never going to get blessed until he admitted one word. It was the one word he had been hiding from his whole life: *Jacob.*

There it was: Jacob's moment of brokenness. It also was his prayer of repentance. All that needed to be said was said, in that one, painful word.

And he said unto him, What is thy name? And he said, Jacob. Genesis 32:27.

After that repentant declaration, there are no further instances of deception attributed to Jacob recorded in the Holy Bible. Jacob was a changed man.

The funny part is he always was the child of promise. God had ordained a remarkable story for him, and declared it his story while he was still in the womb, fighting his twin brother and trying to win his battles on his own.

Two nations are in thy womb, and two manner of people shall be separated from thy bowels; and the one people shall be stronger than the other people; and the elder shall serve the younger. Genesis 25:23.

But he was never going to get that promise until he owned up—albeit painfully—to his name. After Jacob's one-word repentance, the angel renamed him Israel. Israel means a prince who has prevailed with God and men. Jacob had to be weak to become strong. Weakness is a necessary step for each and every pilgrim's progress.

For when I am weak, then am I strong. 2 Corinthians 12:10.

Honesty hurts. Just because you have to repent doesn't mean you have to like it. But you will have to do it. The last two chapters have been as unpleasant for you to read as they have been for me to write.

You can run from it, hide from it, pretend it doesn't exist and bluff your way through it, but until you admit who you really are—who you really, *really* are—you cannot become who you were born to be. This is repentance, and lies at the true heart of what it means to be a Christian.

I guess what I'm saying is you could choose to be offended by what I've written and throw this book away. But there is another way to look at these writings: This could be your moment, your time for new beginnings.

This could be your Jacob moment.

A broken and a contrite heart, O God, thou wilt not despise. Psalm 51:17.

LAST WORDS

O Lord God Almighty, the creator of the heavens and the earth, I have made a mess of doing things my own way, and I wanted to tell you that I am sorry. I want you to lead my path from now on. I choose to follow your words as my guide to life. I, therefore, choose Jesus Christ, your only begotten Son, as my Lord and Guide. I now understand that Jesus Christ, the Word of God, is all of your instructions put together in one man. I choose to follow the Word of God not by my might, nor by my power, but by the guidance of your Holy Spirit. Amen.

THE STORYTELLER
PART "FOUR:" THE TOOLBOX

I t was the last day of what had been a most memorable kid's camp meet. Mentally stimulated, the children had learned concepts which, even though their young minds didn't know it yet, would change their lives forever.

Of course they were all physically exhausted. The camp counselor grinned with wicked satisfaction at the memory of brisk hikes and young limbs clinging to the camp's rock wall, swinging ropes and three-legged races. What fun was a camp meet if you couldn't wear out a group of 'tweens?

But they had one more task to perform. For the last time, in what had become a beloved camp ritual over the last few days, someone was going to look in the toolbox.

"Who's going to pick out the last tool? Hmm, who will it be?" The camp counselor's gaze traveled a leisurely path over the waving hands and eager young faces that had come to know and love him over the previous week.

"Ah, Cody." He smiled gently at the wildly waving little fellow, and addressed the rest of the group. "What do you think, guys?"

A collective mock groan went up from the group, but it was not an unkind one.

"Of course, who else could it be?" "Go on, Cody!" "There goes President Cody!"

There was a cheer as the delighted Cody bounded forward to the raggedy hummed strains of "Hail to the Chief," enjoying friendly hair ruffling and back pats as he made his way up front.

The youngster slowed down to a comical stately walk as he approached the chipped, blue metal toolbox and pulled out the last tool, a slightly bulky rolled up piece of paper.

Adopting his most presidential look, he unrolled the paper, gleefully pocketing the pack of M&M chocolates that fell out, to the wistful sigh of the small crowd.

"Senators, friends and fellow countrymen, please lend me your ears. I shall read from the scroll."

The counselor looked over at him in amusement.

"You've got our ears, Mr. President. Can we hear the contents of your scroll now?"

Cody looked down and his young face became serious as he read.

"Learn to love one another, as I have loved you."

The counselor looked at his group of solemn young pilgrims.

"Jesus said that, many years ago. But what does it really mean to love one another?"

"It means taking the time to get to know one another—out there in your homes, schools, and neighborhoods, as you have done here in camp. You *cannot* love people if you don't know them.

"It means remembering to be kind to your sports opponents, whether you win or lose. Remember: Without opponents, you wouldn't have anyone to play with.

"It means helping up your little brother when he trips and falls. He will be grateful to you for the rest of his life, and will do the same for others.

"It means making friends with the shy new kid in your class. You'll make a friend for life, a friend that will help you one day. I was that shy kid once."

"It means patiently playing dolls with your little sister in her make-belief house. If she bites off her dolls' heads because you didn't care enough to teach her differently, what kind of Mom do you think she'll become? It will happen in fewer years than you think.

"It means sharing the good things you've learned with other people. A beautiful kingdom is not much fun if you're the only one in it.

"It means," he said with a knowing glance toward the president, "sharing your pack of M&Ms. I have found they taste better when shared."

Cody hooted with laughter. "I'm not sure that last point is true." Then, with slightly less certainty: "Mr. Adelman, you *are* joking, right?"

The camp counselor looked at him, then at the expectant group of young chocolate hyenas waiting in the wings, an enigmatic smile on his face. They couldn't have known that a pack of M&Ms would be lying on each youngster's pillow as a parting gift when they got back to the dorm that afternoon.

"Now there, Mr. President. You'll never know until you've tried, will you?"

A CHRISTIAN PILGRIM'S TOOLBOX

O Lord God Almighty, the creator of the heavens and the earth, I have made a mess of doing things my own way, and I wanted to tell you that I am sorry. I want you to lead my path from now on. I choose to follow your words as my guide to life. I, therefore, choose Jesus Christ, your only begotten Son, as my Lord and Guide. I now understand that Jesus Christ, the Word of God, is all of your instructions put together in one man. I choose to follow the Word of God not by my might, nor by my power, but by the guidance of your Holy Spirit. Amen.

That short prayer is the entryway to your lively new existence. If you have said it and meant it, welcome!

However, the choice to enter is only the start of what you have signed on for. It's like getting into college. You first choose that school or college in your mind. Then you pass the school's entrance requirements. The requirements to "Life College" all are in the short repentance prayer you just read.

But college is of no use to you if, once in it, you sit and stare dreamily out of the window during all the classes. That only can lead to disaster. You will not only fail to graduate, you also will drop out of college!

The whole reason for college is to get the best training in the field of your choice, graduate, and use what you've learned to positively impact both yourself and society. If you had no intention of actually doing the course work, *you should have stayed home*.

But there are some people who get into college with no plans of doing the course work. They are more interested in the new sphere of social interaction it affords them. For example, a young man goes to Harvard to study law but actually skips all the freshman classes, joins a fraternity and throws beer and cocaine parties every week. He drops out after his first year at that prestigious institution.

Was the young man ever studying law at Harvard? The answer is *no*. He was studying beer and cocaine theory, a course that, to the best of my knowledge, is not on Harvard's curriculum. Some people may insist on calling him a Harvard drop out, but spiritually speaking, he never was in Harvard.

But you are not like that young man, or you would not be still reading this book.

I gave you plenty of places to opt out, but *you're still here*. I think you are an earnest uncompromising seeker of the truth. This book and its tools are for you.

In Life College, your teacher is the Holy Spirit; the duration of your course is the duration of your physical life; the whole course is on Jesus Christ, God's book of instructions; you finish college when you stop breathing, your heart stops beating, and your brain neurons stop firing — physical death, or spiritual sleep; and you graduate into eternal life, where you will take your appropriate place in God's fantastic creation and do the things you were trained to do in Life College!

So, welcome, but we've got a lot of work to do! I have been delegated by the Holy Spirit to share some basic Life 101 courses with you, giving you the foundational tools for your Christian pilgrim's toolbox. I'm so honored to have been given this privilege; I can't wait to share with you some of the tools I've learned!

I'll take you on some classes, but then I'll have to dash across campus to my own classes.

My friends, I'm in Life College, too.

BASIC TOOLKIT 101.1

Tool Number One: Repentance
Tool Number Two: Prayer
Tool Number Three: Baptism
Tool Number Four: Fasting
Tool Number Five: Tithing
Tool Number Six: Grace, Faith, and Works
Tool Number Seven: Holy Communion and Oil Anointing
Tool Number Eight: The Sabbath

REPENTANCE

You cannot give what you do not have.

I'm sharing with you the bedrock of my own life, the first tool in my toolbox: Repentance. It all begins with repentance. Get hold of a Bible; you will need it for the reference verses.

Repentance means changing your allegiance and making a *covenant* with God to follow his instructions, as they are revealed to you. A covenant is a contract in which only one party has the power to set its terms. It is, therefore, an "all or nothing" contract and is non-negotiable.

Key statement: Do all good instructions.

Depart from evil, and do good; and dwell for evermore. Psalm 37:27.

Let's work through the reasoning process: Without instructions, furniture cannot be put together. Appliances cannot be operated, cars cannot be driven, and destinations cannot be reached in a timely manner, if at all.

If instructions are not followed and we try to perform tasks based on our limited knowledge or "wing it," we usually end up with undesirable results.

Proper instructions are, therefore, necessary to get good results.

1. Jesus Christ of Nazareth is the Word of God, which really means the sum total of all the instructions of God the Father. He is *every* instruction God the Father ever has said about life, from the beginning to the end of time.

(Revelation 1:8; Revelation 22:13; Revelation 19:15; Revelation 19:13; Ephesians 6:17; Hebrews 4:12; John 1:1; John 12:47-50)

2. Jesus Christ, being all God's instructions, is all good instructions, because God is *good*.

(James 1:17; Psalm 145:9; Luke 18:19; Psalm 31:19; Psalm 143:10)

3. Jesus comes forth from and is an exact mirror of his Father, making him both God's Son and God. He is the first and only person made this way, making him the first-born, only begotten Son of God.

(Hebrews 1:3; John 3:16; Psalm 2:7; John 14:9; Romans 8:29; Colossians 1:15)

4. The statement "Jesus Christ is my Lord" means that *you are his servant*.

(2 Peter 1:1; Revelation 1:1-3; James 1:1; Jude 1:1; Titus 1:1; Philippians 1:1)

5. A lord gives instructions, all of which are carried out by his servants. Therefore, accepting Christ as your Lord really means committing to follow all his instructions—*all good instructions*—as when they are revealed to you.

(Luke 17:7-10; Ecclesiastes 12:13; Mark 11:1-7; Psalm 37:27; Luke 9:1-2, 6; Luke 9:14-15; Luke 12:42-47; Luke 14:17-24; Luke 20:9-12)

6. Your covenant payment is the heritage of a son or daughter in your Lord's household. *You co-own the inheritance of the very Christ you serve.*

    (John 1:12; Galatians 3:26; John 4:34-36; Romans 8:16-17; Matthew 5:9; Galatians 4:1-7; 1 John 3:1; Romans 8:21)

7. Why this astonishing payment? Because this was God's initially designed inheritance for all people. Unfortunately, our ancient parents opted out of the "responsibilities" clause of this heritage—God's instructions for living—with deadly results.

    (Genesis 2:7; Deuteronomy 8:3; Matthew 4:4; Luke 4:4; Genesis 2:17; Genesis 3:4-6; Romans 5:12)

If your Christianity professes Jesus Christ as Lord with your lips, but does not include following good instructions when they are given to you, this is not Christianity. You have been party to a different covenant! Your covenant position may be indistinguishable from the righteousness of Pharisees or the "Christianity" of demons.

Therefore to him that knoweth to do good, and doeth it not, to him it is sin. James 4:17.

Pharisees were religious teachers of Jewish law in Israel at the time of Christ. Knowledgeable of God's commandments, they only obeyed God's Word when it suited them, ignoring it the rest of the time.

(Matthew 5:20; Luke 12:1; Matthew 23:1-3; Mark 7:6-13; Luke 11:42; Luke 13:14-16; Luke 18: 10-14; John 8:3-9; James 4:17)

Demons are Satan's band of fallen angels. They know who Jesus Christ is. However, despite all their acknowledgement of God and Jesus Christ as God's Son, demons have a universal theme: *Leave us alone, to do what we want to do.*

(Luke 4:34; Luke 4:41; Luke 8:28; Acts 16:16-18; James 2:19; 1 Peter 2:4; James 4:17)

Let us do a self-searching exercise. Look at the statements below. Do they accurately describe the fullest boundaries of your Christian doctrine?

Jesus is the Son of God, the Most High God (Luke 4:34; Luke 8:28).
Jesus Christ is the Holy One of God (Luke 4:34).
I know that Jesus is the Christ and Messiah (Luke 4:41).
Jesus Christ is the way of salvation (Acts 16:16-18).
Jesus is the Savior and salvation, *which includes death on the cross, resurrection, remission of sins, etc.* (Luke 4:41; Acts 16:16-18).
I fear the one and only God (James 2:19).

All the statements above were made by *demons.*
The Pharisees were religious leaders who said good things, but did something else. Demons are fallen angels who really know God and his Word, but do something else.

Spiritually speaking, they both do *the same thing.*

In other words, if you have learned lots of good things and don't do them, you are in this boat. You need more than this to be a Christian.

Key statement: You *say* what you know, but you *do* what you believe.

The missing ingredient from your toolkit is the under-standing and belief that Jesus Christ is *the Word of God.* Therein lies the power of God: in the things he has said. True Christianity only is achieved by carrying out the good instructions you already have been given.

Christ the power of God, and the wisdom of God. 1 Corinthians 1:24.

Based on your own understanding of what you have just read—whether or not you had previously classified yourself as a Christian—are you a Christian?

O Lord God Almighty, the creator of the heavens and the earth, I have made a mess of doing things my own way, and I wanted to tell you that I am sorry. I want you to lead my path from now on. I choose to follow your words as my guide to life. I, therefore, choose Jesus Christ, your only begotten Son, as my Lord and Guide. I now understand that Jesus Christ, the Word of God, is all of your instructions put together in one man. I choose to follow the Word of God not by my might, nor by my power, but by the guidance of your Holy Spirit. Amen.

Depart from evil, and do good; and dwell for evermore. Psalm 37:27.

LAST WORDS ON REPENTANCE

What is the difference between a servant and a son?

A son works for his own household, and reaps all the benefits of his labor. A servant works for a household and is paid a wage for his services. In terms of the work, *both are indistinguishable*.

A son is a servant who inherits his home.

PRAYER

You now are part of a two-way conversation—in God's language.

This is the second member of your toolkit. Simple to use, prayer is amazingly effective when applied correctly. Learn it well; it avails much. You might as well invest in a Bible— you're going to need it for the lessons.

Prayer, first, is a discussion with God in his language. You speak, he replies.

A boomerang, on the other hand, is a precisely crafted piece of wood that returns to its sender after it has been thrown.

Key statement: Send God's words back to him.

God sends out his words, they accomplish their task, and then they report back to him. God's words are like a returning boomerang; they *must* return to their sender.

So shall my word be that goeth forth out of my mouth: it shall not <u>return unto me void</u>, but it shall accomplish that which I please, and it shall prosper <u>in the thing</u> whereto I sent it. Isaiah 55:11.

Let's see how this works.

The world's first-known flying machine, the boomerang, is the predecessor of the airplane, blimp, helicopter, and space shuttle.

A boomerang needs both a *thrower* and *wind* to return to its sender. The wind is created by the boomerang itself as it slices through still air. A boomerang thrown in a vacuum, therefore (i.e., without wind), *will not return to its sender.*

In terms of its usefulness, it is unclear why the returning boomerang was made. It is a strange invention for ancient people preoccupied with hunting and/or gathering, as it is useless for either activity.

1. God the Father's boomerang is *his Word*. All God's words put together are the spirit of Jesus Christ of Nazareth.

    (John 1:1; John 1:14-17)

2. True Christians are *the wind*. The wind brings change and life. Even breath is wind, as it is *moving air!*

    (John 3:8; Genesis 2:7; John 20:22)

3. God made *everything* by speaking words; therefore, for every circumstance we encounter, there *must* be a specific set of words or instructions. *There are no impossible problems.*

    (Philippians 4:13; Mark 9:23; Joshua 10:12-13; Mark 14:36)

4. God sends out his words, they accomplish their task, and then they report back to him; the Father's words *have to* return to him.

    (Isaiah 55:11; John 16:28; John 20:17-19, 21-22)

5. The wind created by the boomerang returns it to its sender. In like manner, we are created by God's words and are designed to return the Father's words to him. Remember: The spirit of man is a *word container*.

(Revelation 8:4; Ecclesiastes 12:7; John 19:30, Luke 23:46; Revelation 5:8, Psalm 141:2)

6. *The Holy Spirit* teaches us which words to return to God the Father, for each circumstance we encounter.

(Matthew 10:19-20; John 14:26; Romans 8:26; John 16:13-14; 2 Timothy 3:16)

7. The boomerang is not the only time Christ has been symbolized as a miraculous piece of wood in the Bible.

(Exodus 15:23-26; Genesis 7:21-23; 2 Kings 6:1-7; Exodus 25:10-16)

The power in prayer is in what God will do, usually through you, when you close the spiritual loop by sending his words back to him.

So, why this whole process of prayer, anyway?

God is a living God.

(2 Kings 19:4; Psalm 42:2; Matthew 16:16; Mark 12:27)

God moves and breathes. These are two traits that characterize all life, and are given as a token of life to all living creatures made by God. But God the Father does not breathe air.

When the Bible describes a pleasant odor, savor that God enjoys, or God smelling something, God is *inhaling*. When we hear of God's breath or speech, he is *exhaling*.

What does God breathe?

He breathes in prayer, along with other forms of worship.

(Philippians 4:18; Revelation 5:8; Ephesians 5:1-2; Revelation 8:4; Genesis 8:20-22)

He breathes out life, order, blessings, and favor.

(Genesis 8:20-22; 2 Samuel 22:16, Psalm 33:6; Job 37:10; Ezekiel 37:5; Isaiah 42:5)

Blessings go to everybody—both good and bad, including sunshine, seasons, rain, etc.

Favor is given specifically to those who worship him. Favor usually shows up as miracles—extraordinary blessings or, as I like to call them, "Wow!" moments.

So, we have been tasked with the unique privilege and responsibility of worshipping God through prayer, and being the wind of change in the world.

PRAYER LOGISTICS

Collaborative tasks require speaking to one another in the same language. Therefore, the amount of vocabulary you share with God determines how many tasks you can complete in the world he created.

In Life College, you are a trainee, or apprentice. Another word for you is disciple. Prayers are conversations with God, with you *as a trainee*.

Learn to use God's language in the situations you encounter, the same way an apprentice car mechanic talks to the master mechanic about issues he encounters while training on the job. Discussions with his mentor are littered with terms like "crank shaft," "spark plugs," and "carburetor," and not words like "elephants," "tacos," or "Mummy!"

Learn God's vocabulary. Then use the right words in the right place.

PRACTICAL APPLICATION

Try the example below if you or anyone you know is sick. I and several friends of mine have done this many times with excellent results.

1. Sing a couple of choruses. I like to sing these two, but you can say them if you don't know the tunes. Or, pick your own choruses.

   Not by might, nor by power,
   But by my spirit, says the Lord,
   Not by might, nor by power,
   But by my spirit, says the Lord,
   This mountain shall be removed, (say 3 times)
   By my spirit says the Lord.

   Only believe, only believe,
   All things are possible,
   Only believe,
   Only believe, only believe,
   All things are possible,
   Only believe.

2. Have the sick person make this statement of declaration.

   "By your stripes, Lord Jesus, I am healed."

3. Give God thanks, and then reaffirm the statement yourself.

"Thank you, heavenly Father, for this wonderful day and time. I join my voice to (sick person's), agreeing that by your stripes, Lord Jesus, (sick person) is healed."

4. Specify that you are sending God's words back to him and quote Isaiah 55:11.

"I am sending your words back to you, Lord God, because you have said that your words will not return to you void, but must do that for which they were sent."

5. Give thanks to God, closing out the prayer.

That's it. Try it; it works!

The effectual fervent prayer of a righteous man availeth much. James 5:16.

LAST WORDS ON PRAYER

Prayer to God can be God's words spoken, sung, or acted out. Don't get too hung up on the form of prayer. Just use the right words, and believe they will work.

Come boldly before God in prayer. Not arrogantly, but boldly, as children go to their parents with requests. *You have a right to be there.*

Lastly, when all else fails, just throw up your hands and cry: "Jesus, help!" It's not what you went all the way to Life College to learn, but it will get you out of trouble in a pinch. The worst thing that can happen is God says, "Shush!" and then helps you. Is that so terrible?

Let us therefore come boldly unto the throne of grace, that we may obtain mercy, and find grace to help in time of need. Hebrews 4:16.

BAPTISM

It is time to publicly declare who you are.

A very interesting tool, baptism is primarily a showcase to reveal who you are to the public.

This creates some interesting dynamics. You are viewed differently and work more effectively, because baptism gives you a mantle of authority you previously did not have.

Baptism is derived from the original Greek word *baptizo*, and has the same root word as overwhelmed: *whelm*. You are submerged completely—or, quite literally, overwhelmed—usually with water.

A uniform, on the other hand, is an outfit or item usually worn that identifies to the public what you do.

Key statement: Wear your uniform in public for the first time.

Symbolically, baptism is a public ceremony of a private commitment you had made previously. Baptism is your "I'm all in!" statement. It is a formal wearing of your uniform for the first time.

Let's try to explain this.

In the police academy, the police cadets are trained in all the techniques necessary to become good policemen.

A cadet graduates after acquiring a set of physical and mental skills at the police academy. The newly qualified cadet has met all the requirements to be a policeman.

But everybody knows that the cadet stops being "Jimmy from next door" and becomes a police officer the day he wears his policeman's uniform and starts walking the beat.

1. Symbolically speaking, there are three types of baptism discussed in the Bible.

   (Mark 1:8; Matthew 20:22-23)

2. The baptism of repentance was carried out by John the Baptist and, later on, the disciples of Jesus. This symbolizes the internal changes of a truly repentant mind.

   (Mark 1:8; Luke 3:8; John 4:2; 1 Peter 3:21)

3. The baptism of the Holy Spirit is given by Jesus Christ. It symbolizes the Holy Spirit dwelling inside the true Christian believer.

   (John 1:29-34; Acts 2:32-33; John 20:21-22)

4. The baptism of death and resurrection was received by Jesus Christ. It symbolizes eternal self-sacrifice (death), and eternal life with a God-shared inheritance (resurrection).

   (Mark 10:38-40; Acts 12:2-11; John 12:23-24, 27-28; Romans 6:3)

5. All three baptisms are related. They showcase distinct aspects of God's kingdom: *entry* (repentance), *empowerment* (Holy Spirit), and *selfless service with a living inheritance* (self-sacrifice and resurrection).

   (John 10:9; John 3:3; Luke 4:14-15; Hebrews 9:24-26; Philippians 2:5-11)

6. The three baptisms occur sequentially in the Bible: the baptism of repentance first, then Holy Spirit baptism, and lastly, the baptism of self-sacrifice and life.

(Luke 3:21-22; Matthew 20:22-23; Luke 12:50)

7. Today (i.e., since Jesus Christ's ascension to heaven), the three baptisms are meant to be represented in the one baptismal ceremony. The apostle Paul helps us understand this.

(Acts 19:2-7; Romans 6:3-4; 1 Corinthians 15:29-32)

Paul introduces the idea that the baptism of repentance is not enough. It should include being baptized into Jesus Christ and receiving the gift of the Holy Spirit (Acts 19:2-7). The same Paul indicates that baptism into Christ also means being baptized into his death and resurrection (Romans 6:3-4; 1 Corinthians 15:29-32).

Paul merges all three baptisms into one ceremony.

THE BAPTISMS OF JESUS CHRIST

Jesus received his first baptism by John the Baptist, which really symbolizes the mind that has chosen God.

His second baptism was of the Holy Spirit as he stepped out, *praying*, from the baptismal waters of the River Jordan. What was he praying for? The baptism of the Holy Spirit, which his Father freely gives to those who ask him! Being the firstborn of his Father's children, Jesus modeled how this is obtained, and received the full measure of the Holy Spirit.

His third baptism started the day that he died on the cross. This is why Jesus described himself and his Father as glorified at what would appear to be a very inglorious hour!

The death part of that third baptism was fulfilled when he said, "It is finished," and shortly afterwards, died.

The resurrection part of his third baptism started on resurrection day. It ended when he ascended back to our Father, in heaven, to sit at his right hand, serve as our eternal high priest, and inherit all things.

WHY BAPTISM?

- It publicly declares worship and allegiance to God. God wants you to be as proud of him as he is of you, and not ashamed of him!

    (Mark 8:38; Luke 9:26; Matthew 10:26-27, 32-33)

- Declaring God's works before men is your testimony. This is what leads other people to salvation and overcomes Satan.

    (Hebrews. 13:16; Revelation 12:11)

- God is glorified, showcasing how his kingdom works. Everything God the Father created was first a mind decision before it made it outward to creation. Being made in his image, you glorify him by going through the same process.

- It is part of your uniform of righteousness. People need to know who you are, so they know whom to ask for help, and get saved. At least, Jesus seemed to think so.

    (Matthew 3:14-15; Revelation 19:8; Isaiah 61:10; Matthew 10:26-27).

It is a confidence booster. It helps you better articulate who you are in Christ.

BAPTISMAL LOGISTICS

True repentance, borne out by its fruits, is a must before baptism. John the Baptist describes these fruits: materially helping the poor, desisting from violence, anger, cheating, slander, and the discontent that springs from seeing yourself as a perpetual victim (Luke 3:7-14; Matthew 3:7-10).

Baptism is done in the name of Jesus Christ. This symbolizes Christ is your Lord, by whom we receive the free gift of the Holy Spirit. The baptized person should pray for the Holy Spirit baptism *during* their baptism, as Jesus did (Luke 3:21; Acts 19:4-5; Matthew 28:19).

Total submersion in water is necessary. This no longer becomes a point of debate once we grasp the significance of death and resurrection in baptism.

PRACTICAL APPLICATION

1. From the perspective of the baptist, have a baptism class. Discuss the true nature of baptisms, all three of them, and essentially all the stuff we covered above. During this class be sure to discuss the fruits of repentance, so as to avoid ineffective baptisms.

   a. Your baptismal statement could go something like this: "To the glory of Almighty God and in accordance with his Holy Word, I baptize you in the name of the Father, the Son and the Holy Spirit. Amen."

   b. Aim to achieve total submersion in water. Don't
      hesitate to *do it again,* if this was not achieved on
      the first try. Better to repeat it and have its true
      meaning honored, than do a botched job rushing
      through it.

2. From the perspective of the one to be baptized, ensure
   you are truly repentant and ready to follow Jesus as
   Lord, and do not just fake it. Understand that in your
   water baptism, a Holy Spirit baptism is not only
   sought for, *it also is expected.* Pray for the baptism of
   the Holy Spirit, in the same way Jesus did, once you
   emerge from the water something like this: "Thank
   you, heavenly Father, for this opportunity to honor
   you. Lord Jesus, please baptize me with your Holy
   Spirit, as you promised. Amen."

Understand that baptism of the Holy Spirit presents in
different ways. The whole idea is a public display in a language the observing audience can understand. Jesus had a
splitting open of the sky, a dove descend on him, and the
voice of God the Father himself, announcing and loving him
(Matthew 3:13-17; Luke 3:21-22).

The one hundred and twenty apostles had a rushing wind
in a closed room, actual *fire* on top of their heads, and the
sudden collective ability to speak multiple languages they
did not know. This actually was a fulfillment of previous
prophecy (Matthew 3:11; John 3:8; Acts 1:8; Mark 13:10).

Paul, a Pharisee prior to his Christian conversion, had
actual scales drop off his blind eyes after his Holy Spirit
baptism, a visual testimony to his one-man audience, a disciple called Ananias (Acts 9:17-18). This fulfilled a prophecy
about Pharisees.

For judgment I am come into this world, that they which see not might see; and that they which see might be made blind. John 9:39.

Certain men Paul baptized spoke in various languages *and* prophesied (Acts 19:2-7). My baptism was my being suffused in bright light in a very dark room, caught on camera, three days and three nights after my water baptism, symbolic of sharing Christ's death and resurrection baptism.

The whole point is the Holy Spirit will put his stamp on the ceremony and put on a show! I can't wait to hear of how he shows up for you!

Jesus also being baptized, and praying, the heaven was opened, And the Holy Ghost descended. Luke 3:21-22.

LAST WORDS ON BAPTISM

We indicated earlier that baptism showcases entry, empowerment, service, and inheritance in God's kingdom. Let's closely examine these statements Jesus made about himself, in the Gospel of John.

I am the door. John 10:9. (Entry)

The Spirit of truth... he shall testify of me. John 15:26. (Empowerment)

I am the way, the truth, and the life. John 14:6. (Service and sacrifice; living inheritance)

Baptism is all about Jesus.

FASTING

It's all about people.

This tool has been pushed largely into obscurity by Western society, but, if used correctly, this "stone which the builders rejected" is one of the most powerful tools in your toolkit.

Why fast? Because fasting is like Waldo in the *Where's Waldo?* series that began in the 1980s: He has an uncanny knack of appearing in all the fun pictures.

- Moses *fasted* forty days and forty nights in a mountain while he collected the Ten Commandments, the backbone of religious belief in both Judaism and Christianity.

(Exodus 34:28)

- Three nations simultaneously tried to eliminate Southern Israel. King Jehoshaphat and his Jewish nation won without raising a sword in battle. The Jewish people *fasted* before the battle's showdown.

(2 Chronicles 20:3)

- Esther, a Jewish queen of Persia, *fasted* for three days and nights to prevent the genocide of all Jews in the Persian Empire, and succeeded in getting the death order rescinded.

(Esther 4:15-16)

- Anna, a holy prophetess of God, was given the unique honor of announcing who the baby Jesus Christ really was to the Jewish people, at Jesus' birth. The Bible says she *fasted routinely* in the temple, day and night.

(Luke 2:36-37)

- Jesus *fasted* for forty days and forty nights before he started a miraculous ministry so powerful that it birthed the Christian faith.

(Matthew 4:2)

- Saul, who became the apostle Paul, *fasted* as he was instructed by God for three days and three nights before he was baptized and received the Holy Ghost; this is the man who wrote two thirds of the Bible's New Testament.

(Acts 9:9)

- A man from Rome called Cornelius was *fasting* when he was visited by an angel. Through that angelic visit, the baptism of the Holy Spirit discussed in the last section became available to non-Jews for the first time.

(Acts 10:30)

Fasting keeps good company. It's good to have famous friends. One day, you might be famous, too.

Fasting is willful self-sacrifice, including abstinence from food and/or drink for a period, as a means of solving problems.

Compassion is the feeling you have when loved ones are hurt. *Compassion is the look of love.*

What does fasting have to do with compassion? *Everything.* Look at a simple example.

Soldiers who have been deployed to fight in wars are trained to look enemy combatants in the eye and kill without batting an eyelid. But these hardened warriors frequently are undone by the sight of the small, young, starving casualty of war, whose only crime was to be a child in the wrong place at the wrong time.

And so, hard men will forgo their next meal, giving the ration pack to that starving little mite as compassion rears her noble head in the most unlikely of places: a soldier's heart.

But fasting extends its boundaries beyond just the food and drink of this example. If done correctly, fasting is the purest form of complete self-sacrifice you can give this side of eternity. For a predetermined period of time, fasting gives of your *whole self:* body, soul, and spirit.

Key statement: Fasting is the complete self-sacrifice.

Greater love hath no man than this, that a man lay down his life for his friends. John 15:13.

In the Christian, fasting is driven by love and compassion. Let's see how this works. The whole rationale of fasting is addressed beautifully in Isaiah 58:1-12. I highly recommend reading this whole block of verses, to really *get* fasting.

1. Take what is meant for your body and give it to somebody else's body. Give the meal(s) you would have eaten to someone else.

(Isaiah 58:7)

2. Take what is meant for your mind and give it to somebody else. Give spiritual instruction (any good instructions) to those who are hungry for righteous-

ness (the inquisitive mind), or those who are down-cast (depressed or anxious people).

(Isaiah 58:10)

3. Use your free spirit to obtain freedom for other human spirits. Pray specifically for people or groups of people that are spiritually oppressed or in spiritual bondage.

(Isaiah 58:8; Matthew 17:14-21)

4. The rewards of fasting include rapid improvement in health, rapid replies from God to prayers, astuteness, and an honored name and legacy that is carried on by your descendants. In other words, fasting is an acce-lerant for all the good things we want for ourselves and our children.

(Isaiah 58:8-12)

5. God starts your fast's rewards *fast*—i.e., during your physical life, here and now—and publicly, but only if you conduct your fast privately, without any outward fanfare.

(Matthew 6:16-18, Isaiah 58:8-12)

Fasting is, therefore, not to be walked by and dismissed lightly. It is usually not about your personal problems, but somebody else's. It is not to train the mind to get used to a lack of glucose.

Fasting is selfless, not selfish. It's usually not about you; it's about them.

FASTING LOGISTICS

Pick your fasting duration ahead of time. It is not terribly important how long it is; it should just be longer than your usual time between meals.

Pick the spiritual target of your fast ahead of time. Make it as specific as possible: Pick a particular person, group of people, or nation whom you know is/are spiritually oppressed, and pray for God's mercy upon them, as well as his spiritual deliverance for them.

Look around *with expectancy* during your fast to share some nugget of wisdom you possess with someone else. You are particularly looking for "hungry" or inquisitive minds and the "afflicted soul:" the depressed and/or excessively anxious individual (Isaiah 58:10).

Find somebody to whom you can give your missed meals. Homeless shelters such as the Salvation Army are excellent, safe places to do this, though God will call you from time to time to go to a homeless person on a roadside bench.

PRACTICAL APPLICATION.

Here is a practical example and application of fasting. I'll give you my typical routine.

1. My usual fast is from 6 a.m. to 6 p.m., but this varies-from 6 a.m. to noon, done with my young children, to three consecutive 6 a.m.-to-6 p.m. days. No forty-day fasts for me yet.

2. I usually will start with a brief prayer of intent in the morning.

3. Since I eat twice a day, I'm sacrificing one meal: breakfast. My wife will pop my usual breakfast components in a little brown bag, and drop them off at our local Salvation Army. They are always grateful for the food.

4. During the course of my fasting day, I will deliberately look for someone — an inquisitive, depressed or anxious mind — with whom to share some nuggets of wisdom. I almost always find one at work.

5. I will end the fast with a brief prayer of thanksgiving, plus or minus a couple of praise songs, when I get home that evening.

That's it, guys. It's time for a sumptuous dinner, fit for a king! That little routine has served me well over the years.

The latest blessing was my short-sighted younger child receiving miraculous healing of his eyesight after the family fasted and essentially had a late breakfast at noon. That was last month. There's old "Wally" again! He just keeps turning up around the fun stuff, doesn't he?

I Daniel understood… And I set my face unto the Lord God, to seek by prayer and supplications, with fasting. Daniel 9:2-3.

LAST WORDS ON FASTING

Look again at those blessings that go with fasting, from Isaiah 58: good health, peace of mind, wisdom, honor, respect, and bequeathing a noble heritage to your children. Don't you recognize what is happening? *You have become a king.*

This is only fitting, because complete self-sacrifice is what kings do. Self-sacrifice is what love is all about.

God the Father did it. Jesus Christ did it. So, whenever you do it? You show love and, therefore, receive the honor of kings. God uses your life as a noble snapshot in time of his eternal kingdom, because God *is* love (1 John 4:8).

He that hath pity upon the poor lendeth unto the LORD; and that which he hath given will he pay him again. Proverbs 19:17.

TITHING

Give unto God what is God's.

Tithing is the fuel tank of Christian work in the earth and is, therefore, a somewhat pungent-smelling but useful tool. As we will see below, tithing not only helps us keep God's promises; it also enables God to keep his promise to the human race.

Tithing is the giving of God's money to be used for his purposes.

Offerings are the giving of your own money to be used for God's purposes.

Key statement: Everybody owes God tithes.

And I mean: everybody! Nobody is excluded; remember that *the tithe was never your money.* But what about offerings? Do I have an offering to give? I have a simple puzzle for you.

The borrower is servant to the lender. Proverbs 22:7.

Mr. A *loaned* Mr. B one hundred dollars, because Mr. B had no money of his own.

Mr. C was in dire need of ten dollars. Mr. B *gave* him ten dollars, with the approval of Mr. A.

Who really *gave* Mr. C the money? Was it Mr. A, or his "servant," Mr. B?

1. Tithes provide funding for God's church to spread his word around the world. Figuratively speaking, it is used to run God's "house."

(Malachi 3:10)

2. Tithes are one tenth or ten percent of a person's earnings and/or gifts. This is *non-negotiable* and *independent of amount;* i.e., if a person has only ten dollars to his name, then the tithe is one dollar.

(Hebrews 7:1, 6; Genesis 14:18-20; Genesis 28:22; Leviticus 27:30-32)

3. The ten percent tithe law is the same, regardless of the *quality* of the tithe. If all a man owns is ten rotten apples, then his tithe is one rotten apple.

(Leviticus 27:33)

4. Offerings, on the other hand—"vows" in the Old Testament—are negotiable in terms of amount and quality, and are not mandatory. If you do not have an offering to give for financial or quality reasons, do not give one, rather than pledging an offering dishonestly.

(Leviticus 27:1-9; Acts 5:3-4)

5. To not pay tithes is *stealing.* The "rewards" of stealing are violence and destruction; stealing curses the land you occupy and destroys the nation in which you live!

(Malachi 3:8-9; Proverbs 29:24; Exodus 11:1-2; Nahum 3:1; Exodus 12:35-36; Jeremiah 7:9-15; John 10:10; Isaiah 17:12-14)

6. The rewards of tithing are fruitfulness and material blessings, in both yourself and your nation, during your physical lifetime.

(Malachi 3:10-12)

7. There is one last astounding reward to tithing, which has been hidden in plain sight: *Tithing prevents the destruction of the world, as we know it.*

Tithing saves the world?

Let's work through the reasoning. Grab a snack, take a bathroom break if you need to. This explanation is *deep* and needs full attention to be understood.

Why do people steal? Ultimately, for selfish reasons. They may feel forced into it by hunger; feel morally driven to do it like Robin Hood; or just do it for fun and/or the adrenaline rush, like several kleptomaniac celebrities and Washington politicians. After all is said and done, stealing is all about the thief's wants, needs, or even imagined moral code: Thieves are *takers*.

On the other hand, God and his people are *givers*. Jesus said the commandment of all commandments was to love God and neighbor, which is all about giving. Love is God's way on earth.

The earth was filled with violence. And God looked upon the earth, and, behold, it was corrupt; for all flesh had <u>corrupted his way</u> upon the earth. Genesis 6:11-12.

Selfishness ultimately is what destroyed the earth in Noah's day. The takers took and took until there was nothing left except one godly man and his family. And herein lies a secret of God's creation: One holy man among a multitude of takers is not enough to sustain the land in which he lives. God puts that man and his household away in a safe place, and cleans house (Genesis 6:13, 17-18; Genesis 18:20-33; Genesis 19:12-13, 22; Ezekiel 22:29-30; 1 Kings 19:14-18).

Noah was the only righteous man left. So, the rest of the earth had to go. But after that disaster, God made a covenant with Noah: Never again would the whole world be destroyed by flood. But what did this covenant really mean? *There will never again be just one holy man left, on earth.*

God created the rainbow as a token of him upholding his end of that covenant. But what was included in Noah and his descendants' obligation in the rainbow covenant? Actually, it was the first thing Noah did when he stepped off the ark (Genesis 8:20).

Tithing.

It was an obligatory offering to preserve the integrity of God's "house:" heaven and earth, and all the good that it contains. Giving literally is what makes the world go 'round, and tithing forces us to not be perpetual takers.

TITHING LOGISTICS

You should always give tithes. Think of tithes like a God tax. You may not always be able to give offerings. Think of offerings like political campaign contributions. Take your ten percent tithe "off the top," once you have determined your wage packet and monetary gifts.

Pray that God would reveal to you where to put your tithe money with each check or financial gift. Usually, a large portion will go to your habitual place of worship. However, for your own spiritual growth, God may identify somewhere else to put some of your tithe money to work in his house. The passage below will give you several pointers as to where in God's house to put portions of your tithes.

Then shall the righteous answer him, saying, Lord, when saw we thee an hungred, and fed thee? or thirsty, and gave thee drink? When saw we thee a stranger, and took thee in? or naked, and clothed thee? Or when saw we thee sick, or in prison, and came unto thee? And the King *shall answer… <u>Inasmuch as ye have done it unto one of the least of these my brethren, ye have done it unto me.</u>* Matthew 25:37-40.

If you owe money, you should give tithes only, *not offerings*, **to God's kingdom.** All the earnings of a servant under a particular master belong to that master (Exodus 21:3-4). If you are a debtor and give offerings of what you imagine to be your own money, blessings go to the person or people that really gave the offering (2 Chronicles 1:6-7; 2 Chronicles 7:1; Proverbs 22:7). In your case, that includes… I think you can fill in the blanks. In other words, any person who has not completely paid off their debt—including their portion of their nation's debt—is, technically speaking, not qualified to give an offering.

You can't give what you don't have.

PRACTICAL APPLICATION

I've given tithes for as long as I can remember. However, about three years ago, I became aware that my debts needed to be cast off, rather than tolerated.

I came to understand that my "good" and "bad" debts essentially nullified any God offerings I made. So, I changed my giving practices. I stopped giving offerings to God and stuck with tithes. It has been one of the best decisions I ever made.

This is what I do. You can modify it to suit your circumstances.

1. I took on a second job. This was done to expedite the paying off of all my debts.

2. The tithe money from job Number One goes to my primary church place of worship.

3. I specifically pray to God for direction on were to plant the tithe money from job Number Two. For three years, God has not failed to show me a place of acute need in his house. Rarely have I given to the same place twice.

I still owe money, but it is less than half of what it used to be! Imagine that: Getting rid of almost two thirds of your debt, during a global recession! Financially, I have done better in the last three years than at any time in the preceding ten. By God's grace, I will get this albatross off my back soon. With proper tithing, so can you.

Prove me now herewith, saith the LORD of hosts, if I will not open you the windows of heaven, and pour you out a blessing, that there shall not be room enough to receive it. Malachi 3:10.

LAST WORDS ON TITHING

The statistics show that less than ten percent of regular churchgoers pay tithes. But as I have been saying all book long, going to "church" does not a Christian make. There are essentially two types of people in the world: givers and takers. Which one are you?

Remember the words of the Lord Jesus, how he said, It is more blessed to give than to receive. Acts 20:35.

WORKS IN THE KINGDOM OF GOD

A miracle is a finished work.

The "works" tool has been the subject of some debate as to its place in the kingdom of God. The place of works has been questioned in the presence of another component of God's kingdom called *grace*.

We then, as workers together with him, beseech you also that ye receive not the grace of God in vain. 2 Corinthians 6:1.

Grace is the unmerited favor given by a person or persons. In the context of this discussion, grace is the unearned favor of God. Grace is a gift, not a wage.

An orchard is a farm that exclusively grows fruits or nuts.

So, is it grace versus works, or grace *and* works? Let's see if we can sort this out with a simple illustration.

Mr. Potential had wanted an orchard for about as long as he could remember. Unfortunately, he was poor and unskilled in farming of any kind.

One day, Potential got a letter in the mail from a certain Mr. Grace. It contained the title deed to an orchard and a brief note telling Potential that he was being given the opportunity to realize his dream.

Delighted and surprised, Potential ran to his dream orchard, saw beautiful fruit trees in full bloom, a beaming smiling teacher, and lots of shiny new tools for harvesting and planting waiting for him. Overjoyed, he sat down on the ground, looking at the trees, tools, and teacher. And there he sits, to this very day.

Grace gave Potential an orchard to work in. But what use is Potential's orchard to him if he does no work?

For we are his workmanship, created in Christ Jesus unto good works, which God hath before ordained that we should walk in them. Ephesians 2:10.

Key statement: You must have good works to be in the kingdom of God.

The key to works in the kingdom of God is not *if* you do the works, but *how* you do the works. Let's look at the standard pattern of how things get done, in God's kingdom.

1. Works are done *because of*—and not *in place of*—grace in God's kingdom. We are called upon to hope, believe, and with faith accept that God has extended to us this great invitation to both work and partake in his kingdom.

(Ephesians 2:4-10; James 2:20; Matthew 9:36-38)

Internal thought starts here.

2. A good work starts internally from *good thoughts*. We are instructed to make a conscious effort to think about positive and good things, as our thoughts will determine our subsequent actions.

(Philippians 2:5; Philippians 4:8)

3. Next comes *hope*. We hope that a good thought will come to pass. We *must* hope: We are saved by hope; the absence of hope is despair, and all is lost.

(Romans 8:24)

4. Then comes *belief*. At this point, you have gone beyond hope. You actually believe that your good thought can come to pass. Therefore, we align our beliefs with our hopes.

(Mark 9:23)

Up until this point, everything that has happened has occurred within the confines of your head. It is now time to go public.

External action starts here.

5. Next up is *faith*. Game on! This is the risk-taking part. Faith is the tangible substance of things hoped for. Faith is putting observable action to your belief *before* you see your hope come to pass.

(Hebrews 11:1; Hebrews 11:6; Romans 4:16-22)

6. Finally comes the *finished good work*. This usually shows up as a positive outcome called a blessing. Some positive results are extraordinary—or "Wow!" events—and these are called miracles. The finished good work fulfills your hope and validates your faith.

(James 2:17-18)

7. The sole purpose of all grace *every* unearned gift the Holy Spirit brings us—is to do good works for *other people*. In other words, *there is no primarily self-serving gift of the Holy Spirit*.

(2 Corinthians 9:8-9; Romans 1:11; 1 Peter 4:10)

Mr. Potential did fine on Numbers One through Five, with enough faith to visit the orchard site rather than throw his invitation away as a cruel hoax.

But who will enjoy the orchard's beautiful produce if it is not harvested? And how long will Potential own the orchard of his dreams, if he sits on the ground surrounded by tools, and does *nothing*?

But wilt thou know, O vain man, that faith <u>without works</u> is <u>dead</u>? James 2:20.

THE GIFTS OR "TOOLS" OF THE HOLY SPIRIT

It is not my intention to discuss the spiritual gifts in detail, as that is a more advanced spiritual topic than the foundational classes we have been discussing. My intent is more of an overview, with an emphasis on how gifts relate to works in God's kingdom.

1. There are multiple gifts of the Holy Spirit. The first two you get are eternal life and righteousness. Some others that follow are: prophecy, knowledge, wisdom, speaking different tongues or languages, interpretation of tongues, extraordinary perception of spiritual events, healing, extraordinary faith, and the performance of "Wow!" events or miracles.

2. Though freely given, spiritual gifts are tools, not toys. These gifts are given by God's grace, as an *unmerited favor*. However, they are given as tools to carry out good works in God's kingdom, not for personal amusement and/or exclusive personal development.

3. The gifts are situation-specific. Every Christian has the Holy Spirit mingled with their own spirit and,

therefore, has the capacity to receive and manifest all of the spiritual gifts. However, the Holy Spirit only will give you the tools (or gifts) you need to do God's works in your particular sphere of influence. In other words, if you live in a houseboat on a creek, you do not need a shiny new car.

4. Gifts and needs are directly proportional. If you are located in a place of great need, you will be given more gifts, because more works are needed in such a place. Paul the Apostle was delegated to plant the living church in many different nations; therefore, he spoke more languages (tongues) than the average Christian. (1 Corinthians 14:18)

5. The ultimate aim of grace is to create widespread change. Grace-enabled works in God's kingdom have one function only: to change people. A God-directed change of the mind develops godly character in the Christian, and is the first step to entering God's kingdom for the non-Christian. (Romans 1:11)

And God is able to make all grace abound toward you; that ye, always having all sufficiency in all things, may abound to every good work: As it is written, He hath dispersed abroad; he hath given to the poor: his righteousness remaineth for ever. 2 Corinthians 9:8-9.

KINGDOM WORK LOGISTICS

Identify needs in your area of influence: yourself, family, neighbors, the workplace, etc. Start with you and family, working your way outwards like a ripple. You probably will not do great kingdom works in distant places, if you cannot first perform them at home.

Pick the best possible resolution to the identified problem and then, quite literally, hope for the best. Do not compromise your hope; aim high!

Ask God for instructions on how to achieve your hope. This is achieved by prayer. (For details on how to pray, see the prayer section.)

Carefully follow the instructions God gives you, in faith. Then wait expectantly for the finished result.

When the result shows up, make sure that anyone who will listen knows that God performed the miracle. Tell them all about it, including your implementation flubs— in other words, all the gory details! Remember: There is no more powerful tool to overcome Satan and change a mind than your own personal testimony!

And they overcame him by the blood of the Lamb, and by the word of their testimony. Revelation 12:11.

PRACTICAL APPLICATION

Have you ever misplaced a sorely needed document, or your car keys or something? I'm sure you have! I'll give you a really simple technique I use, that you can try yourself at home, to get you started on this "works" thing.

1. I *hope* that I will find the missing item. (At least I hope that I hope that!)

2. I *believe* I will find what is missing. (Or I wouldn't still be looking!)

3. I start singing a praise song to God *out loud,* while still looking, giving God thanks for finding it *before* I find it. (Prayer and faith.)

4. Usually within a minute or so, I'll get a thought of where to look (God's instructions to me) and I'll find the item!

Simple stuff, huh? Some time ago, my girlfriend saw me indulging in this strange behavior and asked what on earth was I doing. So, I told her my very, *very* "uncool" testimony. She gave me a long look and nodded politely. We were dating, after all.

After seeing me do it a few times with great results—and after misplacing a few car keys herself—she started doing it! It worked for her, too; fancy that! I guess she was so grateful, she decided to marry me.

As every man hath received the gift, even so minister the same one to another, as good stewards of the manifold grace of God. 1 Peter 4:10.

LAST WORDS ON WORKS

So, why did I sing a praise song instead of say a prayer? Primarily because praise is a secret weapon. Jesus once told a group of Pharisees that out of the mouth of "babes and sucklings" God had made perfect praise (Matthew 21:16). I think Jesus was just freeing me up to use my singing voice with no worries! But Jesus actually was referring to this psalm, which reads slightly differently.

Out of the mouth of babes and sucklings <u>hast thou ordained strength</u> because of thine enemies, that thou mightest <u>still the enemy and the avenger</u>. Psalm 8:2.

Singing praise establishes spiritual strength: Satan is stopped in his tracks and cannot cause you any havoc while you praise God.

Besides, praise songs are musical prayers with a fixed set of words. Praising prevents the wrong words from slipping out of my mouth, which has been known to happen from time to time. I always keep a couple of "pet" or "go-to" praise songs handy for emergencies.

HOLY COMMUNION
AND ANOINTING WITH OIL

As many as gather in Jesus Christ's name are designated holy ground.

I have put these two tools together because both are symbolic of being recognized as God's people here on earth. They are useful tools in reminding Satan—the great thief—of who we really are, as he likes to act as though he's forgotten. Sometimes, though, we are the ones who need the reminding!

Holy Communion is a ceremony in which Christians gather together and share bread and the "fruit of the vine"—wine or grape juice—in honor of Jesus Christ.

Anointing with oil is when oil is placed on a person and/or thing identifying them as belonging to God, to be used for his purposes.

Key statement: Stand back! I belong to Jesus.

The cup of blessing which we bless, is it not the communion of the blood of Christ? The bread which we break, is it not the communion of the body of Christ? 1 Corinthians 10:16-17.

Thou preparest a table before me in the presence of mine enemies: thou anointest my head with oil. Psalm 23:5.

The message to Satan and his demons is that you have drawn a line in the sand with your big toe, saying, "I belong to Jesus. Don't mess with me!" Oil anointing and Holy Communion, therefore, serve as both remedy and deterrent to the thief and spiritual bully, sort of like this tongue-in-cheek depiction:

A thief broke into a man's house and was unnerved to hear a voice saying repeatedly, "Jesus is watching you!"

He heaved a huge sigh of relief when he discovered the voice came from the homeowner's pet parrot, watching him harmlessly from its cage.

With disdain, the thief scoffed. "What kind of silly homeowner names his pet parrot Jesus?" The parrot calmly answered: "The same kind that calls his pet Rottweiler, Moses."

Enter "Moses," with a spine chilling growl. Oops.

1. The first Holy Communion was done by Christ and his twelve disciples on the first day of a Jewish feast called the Passover.

   (Matthew 26:26-28; Mark 14:22; Luke 22:19-20)

2. The ceremony was a blessing for the eleven disciples that truly followed him. It was a curse for the one disciple who didn't.

   (Matthew 26:23-24; Mark 14:21; Luke 22:21-22)

3. This ceremony is to be done periodically by every Christian. It will be enjoyed with Jesus in person *after* his return from heaven, when God's kingdom has come fully on earth.

   (Matthew 26:29; Mark 14:25; Luke 22:18)

4. Jesus Christ's eternal sacrifice enables God to dwell in the people who choose him, replacing God's previous earthly dwelling places in tabernacles and temples.

(Ephesians 2:19-22; 1 Corinthians 3:16; Exodus 40:34-35; 2 Chronicles 6:41; 2 Chronicles 7:1-2)

5. In ancient times, a sacrificial lamb's blood was sprinkled over the tabernacle/temple priests and their equipment, cleansing and making them holy. Olive oil also was used to anoint these same priests and equipment, establishing them as holy. These two activities are, therefore, similar.

(Leviticus 8:10-13; Exodus 29:21; Hebrews 9:19-22)

6. Holy Communion commemorates Christ's shed blood spiritually cleansing his temple and priests: his followers. Olive oil establishes the holiness of these same temple priests and their "equipment," or implements of influence. Therefore, the oil stands for the blood of Christ.

(1 Corinthians 3:16; 1 Corinthians 5:7-8; Exodus 29:21; Leviticus 8:10-13; Ephesians 2:13-22; Hebrews 10:19)

7. When either of these activities is performed, it is very important we stand in the right place with God. Anything less and we cheapen Jesus' sacrifice, making a mockery of it. We become like the traitorous twelfth disciple and get a curse instead of a blessing.

(1 Corinthians 3:17; 1 Corinthians 11:23-30; Acts 1:16-20)

JESUS CHRIST THE PASSOVER LAMB

The Passover story is about how a sacrificial lamb was killed and its blood placed on the lintels and doorposts of Israelite households while they were enslaved in Egypt. The blood was an external mark of protection over the marked households, so that those households were "passed over" or spared the mass judgment on all other houses in Egypt that claimed the life of all the firstborns in that land. The lamb's meat was eaten with unleavened bread.

Why unleavened? Because unleavened bread is rapidly made; no time is needed for the dough to rise, unlike leavened or yeasty bread. This symbolized the Israelites' rapid departure from Egypt (Exodus 12:8-11, 34, 39; Deuteronomy 16:3).

The original Passover lamb's blood is symbolized by grape products from the "vine," or grapevine. Either grape juice or wine was used, as there was no brandy during Jesus' time. (Matthew 26:26-29; Luke 22:18-20).

This whole process was prophetic of Jesus Christ and the Christian's relationship to him. Jesus was sacrificed and those who mark their "homes" with his blood are passed over, so that a judgment of death does not fall on them. *Jesus Christ is the Passover Lamb.* This is why Isaiah the prophet, John the Baptist, and John the disciple refer to Jesus as the sacrificed Lamb of God (John 1:29, 36; Isaiah 53:7; Acts 8:32-35).

- He is the Word of God and, therefore, he must be spiritually eaten, even as the lamb and the bread of Passover were eaten.

(John 6:51-54; Exodus 12:8-10)

- The newly repentant person has been saved or "passed over" by the blood of Jesus, the Passover Lamb, in the same way the original Passover lamb's blood saved the Israelite slaves in Egypt.

• Christ followers must have a spiritually speedy departure from "Egypt"—the way of current worldly thinking—symbolized during the Passover by the quickly prepared unleavened bread.

(Exodus 12:34, 39; Deuteronomy 16:3; 2 Timothy 2:22; 1 Timothy 6:9-11; 1 Corinthians 10:14)

• The bread is called the bread of affliction: troubles, oppression and ailments. The covenant of the affliction from sin is broken in the Christian. Therefore, as Jesus Christ took all our afflictions on himself and became sin for us, his body also was broken.

(Deuteronomy 16:3; 1 Corinthians 11:24; John 3:14)

• The Christian follows God's instructions—Jesus Christ—and flees from evil, even as the Israelites followed the cloud of God by day and God's pillar of fire by night, as they fled from Egypt.

(Exodus 13:21-22; John 5:14; John 17:14-16; 1 Timothy 6:9-11; 2 Timothy 2:22)

• The Christian is baptized in water symbolizing passing from death to life, as the children of Israel passed through water from death (Egypt) to life (The Promised Land).

(1 Corinthians 10:1-4; Romans 6:3-5)

- Those who have eaten of the Lord's Passover without obeying God's instructions bring judgment and a curse on themselves which, if unchecked, will lead to physical death or spiritual sleep. Many from the first Passover died on the way to the Promised Land. This also happened to oil-anointed priests of God who chose to disobey his instructions.

(Leviticus 10:1-2; 1 Corinthians 10:5-10; 1 Corinthians 11:27-30)

Holy Communion was started by Jesus Christ during the Passover ceremony because it is a continuation and indicates the *same thing*. If the anointing of oil sets the person apart as holy, it does the exact same thing that the sacrificial blood of Jesus does spiritually for the Christian.

Therefore, the anointing of oil is a physical representation of being spiritually covered by the blood of Jesus Christ. The blood of Christ drives away any of Satan's claimed footholds in your life.

HOLY COMMUNION AND OIL ANOINTING LOGISTICS

For Holy Communion: Use grape juice or wine. I also think it is probably more appropriate to use unleavened rather than leavened bread, given what unleavened bread is symbolic of: a rapid exit from worldly ways of thinking and a taking on of the mind of Christ. I'd very much like that to happen to me. Wouldn't you?

For oil anointing: Use olive oil. I don't think one has to be too particular about what brand of olive oil is used; any good cooking olive oil will do. Bless it and place a dab on the forehead, afflicted body part, or inanimate object you want to anoint, briefly stating that this is being done in Jesus Christ's name.

For both activities: Pray before you partake in either one! If there are any obvious impediments in you, such as a feeling of unforgiveness or anger toward anyone, release them in your mind first and forgive them. If there are specific areas of disobedience to God's instructions in your life, take care of those areas first. You want the blessings that come with these activities, not the curse that comes from trivializing them! And don't forget praise songs are musical prayers; I use these during the actual ceremony itself.

PRACTICAL APPLICATION

For Holy Communion, I have always taken Holy Communion in a congregational church setting. The procedure would work well at home too.

1. *I pray first,* releasing anyone I possibly could have anything against and asking God for cleansing in any areas I have fallen short of properly representing him. My prayer usually goes something like this:
Heavenly Father, I praise your holy name. I release anyone I hold anything against right now. I forgive them; they owe me nothing. I am sorry for the places I have stepped outside of your will, both knowingly and unknowingly. I never want to cheapen or forget my Lord and your Son Jesus Christ's sacrifice for me. In the mighty name of Jesus I pray. Amen.

2. I go up and, to the sounds of a praise song, get the piece of bread from the communion worker, breaking the piece in two.

3. I take the proffered grape juice, either in a small cup, or soaked up in the bread.

4. Returning to my seat, I eat the bread and swallow the grape juice.

For oil anointing, I do this with family or sometimes with somebody outside of my family who needs prayers for a physical illness.

1. I pray the same prayer as for Holy Communion.

2. I bless the olive oil, saying that it is set apart for God's purposes.

3. I anoint my forehead with a dab of oil, saying: "I anoint myself in the name of the Father, Son, and Holy Spirit, through Jesus Christ my Lord. Amen."

4. I sing praise hymns, dabbing lintels, doorposts, car hoods, and computers at will 'til I'm satisfied.

5. I usually end with a loud excited shout of: "In the mighty name of Jesus, amen!" I'm excited; I can't help it!

I have used olive oil anointing to extricate myself from a sticky business partnership I unknowingly got into with people who I later found out were Satanists. I learned a valuable lesson from the experience, and use the procedure regularly now, usually about once a month. I also have used olive oil anointing for physical healing in other people, with miraculous results. Satan and his minions are forced to scamper away, as God's soldiers powerfully let Satan know who I really am.

I only have recently understood the unleavened bread part of Holy Communion, from a good Christian friend of mine. I grew up taking unleavened bread communion but recently have been using leavened bread, as that is what is served in most modern congregational churches. I look forward to the great things God will do as I use the information I have learned and shared with you, and go back to my first love!

Take, eat; this is my body. And he took the cup, and gave thanks... Drink ye all of it; For this is my blood of the new testament. Matthew 26:26-28.

For, lo, thine enemies, O LORD... all the workers of iniquity shall be scattered. But my horn shalt thou exalt... I shall be anointed with fresh oil. Psalm 92:9-10.

LAST WORDS ON HOLY COMMUNION AND OIL ANOINTING

Did you know that Jesus is described symbolically in Scripture as a rod (Isaiah 11:1)? In Holy Scripture, a rod or staff makes a covenant, and to break a covenant you must break the rod. That is why Jesus' body was broken by the stripes of a Roman whip on his crucifixion day.

And I will cause you to pass under the rod, and I will bring you into the bond of the covenant. Ezekiel 20:37.

And I took my staff, even Beauty, and cut it asunder, that I might break my covenant which I had made with all the people. Zechariah 11:10.

Moses and Aaron, his brother, had miraculous rods by which they carried out all those miracles in Egypt and later the wilderness. However, Aaron's rod did a strange thing once: It turned into a serpent, swallowing up all the serpents of Egyptian magicians!

For they cast down every man his rod, and they became serpents: but Aaron's rod swallowed up their rods. Exodus 7:12.

If a serpent denotes sin; Egypt, the world; and Jesus is symbolized by Aaron's rod, then all the afflictions of this world were swallowed by Jesus when he became sin on the cross, for our sakes. *That is why you break the bread during Holy Communion.*

THE SABBATH

It's time to take your Sabbath rest.

This is the last of our primary foundational tools for our toolkit. This is not exactly an unknown or new tool; the tradition of the Sabbath is first recorded early in the Bible narrative, in the Second Chapter of Genesis. But it is most recognizable as one of the Ten Commandments. It is part of why weekends are traditionally non-working days.

God said that man should work for six days, and then rest on the seventh day as he had rested. That seventh day is the Sabbath (Exodus 20:8-11).

Let's examine rest and how it relates to people: body, soul, and spirit.

Everybody needs a break. Our bodies and minds cease from work periodically in the process known as sleep.

If a body or mind doesn't get rest, one stops functioning correctly and shuts down the other. Sleep apnea is a disease that causes a breakdown of multiple body areas, from a lack of complete "mind" sleep.

But how does a spirit rest? And did all creation cease to function when God rested on the seventh day?

I guess what I'm asking is how God rested, being a spirit, so that my spirit will know how to rest, too.

Key statement: God is resting in motion.

1. What is Sabbath rest? It is all the activities that God the Father does while he and heaven are resting. Creation continues to live; good activities that promote life are lawful to perform on the Sabbath day.

(Matthew 12:12; John 5:9; John 9:14; Luke 14:5)

2. God the Father and all of heaven—where he resides—currently is still in his seventh day, *resting*.

   (Hebrews 3:11, 18-19; Matthew 11:28; Hebrews 4:1-11)

3. Our spirits are supposed to rest like God does: in motion. We cease from our own works as God did from his.

   (Hebrews 4:10; Isaiah 58:13)

4. Jesus Christ said he is the Lord of the Sabbath. This means the Sabbath day has to agree with what Jesus Christ says is lawful to do on that day: good things for *other people*. Remember: As a servant, the Sabbath day must do what its master says.

   (Matthew 12:8; Mark 1:21)

5. Because of Jesus Christ, we also are *lords of the Sabbath*. Therefore, we do the same things Jesus did on the Sabbath day: good things for other people such as feeding their spirits through teaching, and healing their bodies and minds. These are the activities of a resting spirit on the Sabbath day.

   (Matthew 12:12; Mark 2:23-27; Mark 3:2-4; Luke 4:16; Isaiah 58:13)

6. The dividends of keeping the Sabbath are that God will honor you here on earth; you will enjoy his company as a friend in much of the same way as Enoch and Abraham did; and he will give you a share of Israel's heritage in eternity.

(Isaiah 58:14)

7. The activities of the Sabbath day and of true fasting are very similar in both the specifics of giving and their rewards. This is why Isaiah discussed them together, in the same chapter.

(Isaiah 58:1-14)

In other words: Learn, discuss God's word, and do good things for others on the Sabbath day. You will become nobility, both now and in eternity.

SABBATH LOGISTICS

Decide on what is work for you. It differs from person to person. Hand-washing dishes is not work for me; it relaxes me! That is obviously not the case for everybody.

Stay away from what constitutes work for you. This of course involves a certain amount of planning during the week. Don't keep having an "Oops! I've got to go to work!" moment, on your Sabbath day.

Make a conscious mental decision of intent on your Sabbath to help somebody other than yourself. This could be in any number of ways; just make it something *good*. Honoring the Sabbath day is really not complicated, nor is it difficult. It is actually a day to showcase what you have already been doing all week, as a true Christian, because once you accept Jesus Christ as your Lord, your spirit rests.

For we which have believed do enter into rest. Hebrews 4:3.

PRACTICAL APPLICATION

1. I have found it easiest to kick off the Sabbath day by going to my congregational church. This affords an opportunity to meet a lot of people and scout out for a place to help somebody.

2. I work at the prayer altar while at the church building. People come up from time to time for prayers and advice. Once again, this is an even more specific area to give to people who are in need.

3. At home, I usually will place a call to a specific person or persons, with the sole purpose of sharing a spiritual nugget or two that I have learned over the previous week.

4. Of course, I avoid work on my Sabbath day, if I can help it—and hand-wash dishes, from time to time.

That's my Sabbath day in a nutshell. How about yours?

Come unto me, all ye that labour and are heavy laden, and I will give you rest. Matthew 11:28.

LAST WORDS ON THE SABBATH

The actual day you choose is probably less important than picking a consistent day for your Sabbath.

Scientifically speaking, we now know that your Sunday may be Saturday somewhere else in the world, and the sun doesn't go down for six months at the North and South poles. Some places in the world have Saturday as the last day of the week; others, Sunday.

Besides, how do you know for sure that the day you call the seventh day is actually the seventh day, be it Saturday or Sunday? Were you there on the first day of the world, to know the seventh?

I guess my point is that legalism defeats the whole aim of the Sabbath, making us servants to it and not the other way around. God is honored by perfect intent, not perfect appearance.

The LORD seeth not as man seeth; for man looketh on the outward appearance, but the LORD looketh on the heart. 1 Samuel 16:7.

200 LEVEL TOOLKIT: PRIMER

Well, my friends, you have just waded through the basic building blocks of Christianity, and hopefully you got more than a little wet. Congratulations! I have thoroughly enjoyed sharing every lesson. Sharing them with you has blessed me as much as they have you.

But we have one more concept to discuss before I close out: All of the topics in the basic toolkit had to do with you or I working as a *single unit* to forward God's purposes in his kingdom.

Effective though you have become, you will always be limited as a single unit. Jesus Christ himself fully understood and commented on this limitation during a discussion about his third baptism, even though he was God on earth.

But I have a baptism to be baptized with; and how am I straitened till it be accomplished! Luke 12:50.

The next level is where you learn to work on a team with other Christians. Team activity greatly amplifies individual effort. But as a team player, you now are part of a much bigger picture than you ever were as a single unit.

This primer sneaks a look into your new stomping grounds by introducing you to some spiritual math. *Math?* That's right: addition, subtraction, multiplication, and division, and how they relate to spiritual life systems.

How should one chase a thousand, and two put ten thousand to flight. Deuteronomy 32:30.

ADDITION

Addition: The most rudimentary of mathematical skills, we start addition as infants usually with small fluffy toys and toothless grins. Addition is how we have taught our children vocabulary, by using this simplest of processes: *Door!* That's the big, rectangular thing that opens "outside." *Knob!* That's the small, tubular thing for the hand to push or pull. *Doorknob!* That's door plus knob, the small, tubular or round thing sitting on the big, rectangular thing that opens "outside."

And so on, and so forth. Our secular dictionary words are based exclusively on it; a word is given a meaning, and then has another meaning *added* to it. In other words, we tear out chunks of the unknown, tag these chunks with a title which makes them known, throw them on a vocabulary pile, and keep adding to the pile.

Our thoughts are various combinations of words from this addition-based vocabulary. Our formidable civilization has sprung from sharing this vocabulary, according to set standards, over time.

But we are limited by our words; our endeavors are largely limited to additive thought, because we lack the words to think in terms of anything else. Here are a few examples.

1. Success

> We equate success and blessings with the total number of material possessions owned. Adding material possessions has, therefore, become our yardstick for success.

2. The human spirit

> We have been unable to properly identify the human spirit or other spiritual activity. A spirit's inability to be physically "tagged and bagged" makes it remain unknown.

3. Problem solving

   We solve problems of lack with plans to add more, and rarely by improved efficiency (infrastructure, money, disease treatment, middlemen, "big government," etc.)

4. Simple math

   Our younger generation is increasingly unable to perform simple math more complicated than addition. If you doubt me, please observe the check-out clerk calculating your change at the local grocery.

With addition only, in the big scheme of things, our civilization would be about as sophisticated as a hundred toddlers left unsupervised at a construction site, with the expectation that they will lay concrete.

SUBTRACTION

Now, let us step out of the box for a minute. What if we were to define words by using the slightly more advanced mathematical processs of subtraction?

A word with a known meaning is *subtracted* from another known word to create a new word. Language would now include identifying and naming the difference between the two known words—or *discrepancies*—hence making them known.

Let's look at this example from the Bible's creation story. At first, all that could be seen was a mixture of water and land that looked like water.

The Spirit of God moved upon the face of the waters. Genesis 1:2.

Then, God *subtracted* the water away from the water/ earth watery mix and revealed the discrepancy: land.

And God said, Let the waters under the heaven be gathered together unto one place, and let the dry <u>land</u> appear: and it was so. And God called the dry <u>land</u> Earth. Genesis 1:9-10.

Subtraction opens up a whole new world, because it reveals discrepancies, identifying gaps—something addition cannot do. Subtractive thought mostly improves efficiency by providing immediate solutions, without necessarily increasing size. In other words, it fills the potholes, instead of trying to build a brand new road.

Sometimes, the "pothole" turns out to be an already known word that has not been placed in its proper context. Used in the right place, the word is problem-solving; displaced from its proper context, it is like a jigsaw piece in the wrong place, and ceases to be effective.

Let's take a few examples of additive versus subtractive thought and solutions.

1. The human spirit

   a. In the additive model, the human spirit equals the intangible part of that person. Is this the same as the soul? The mind? What *are* you anyway? *Work based on your body and mind only.*

   b. In the subtractive model, the human spirit equals who the human is—measured by his/her achievements—minus who the human should be—measured by his/her anthropology. *Use the human spirit, mind and body, for much better results.*

2. Jobs

    a. In the additive model, new jobs equals new ideas and (+) new concepts, supported by the addition of (+) new infrastructure. *Create exploratory sub-committees, place contract bids, build infrastructure, and take years.*

    b. In the subtractive model, new jobs equals projected business—how a business ideally should be, based on your business model—minus actual business—how a business is currently. *Create new jobs almost instantly from existing businesses, at a fraction of the cost of laying down infrastructure for new ones.*

3. Anxiety

    a. In the additive model, anxiety equals an abnormal feeling of stress, (+) distraction, (+) worry, and (+) the breakdown of function with or without a triggering environmental event. *Take a pill to anesthetize the gap between the "wannabe" you and "the real" you. If the gap gets bigger, take more pills.*

    b. In the subtractive model, anxiety equals who you think you are—or what you think you can do—minus who you really are—what you really are able to do. The higher your plans exceed your capabilities, the bigger the gap and the worse the anxiety. *Be humble. Reduce your projects to more closely match your capabilities. Anxiety is closely related to pride!*

Subtraction is harder than addition, and is a skill usually acquired at four or five years of age. In other words, with the "addition of subtraction," our civilization leaps in sophistication to kindergarten level. Better, but still not good enough.

MULTIPLICATION

This more advanced math maneuver makes *the same thing occur in different places*. For example:

2 x 4 = 2, added up in four places (2 + 2 + 2 + 2) = 8

As you can see, multiplication is closely related to addition; each unit plays its part which, when added together, makes a much larger whole. Both create solutions, but multiplication is more dynamic. Multiplication is addition on steroids.

Let's look at a well known example of this. God made man and (+) woman.

God blessed them, and God said unto them, Be fruitful, and *multiply*, *and replenish the earth. Genesis 1:28.*

The result? 6.7 billion people currently living on the earth—and counting.

Here's another example of multiplication in action: The recent spread of democracy around the Arab world has used multiplication for effect.

Democracy (the same thing) added up in different countries (different places) = Worldwide changes in social behavior transcending age, race, and gender.

Multiplication needs a connector to string together multiples of the same item. With arithmetical numbers, that connector is the plus sign. With the spread of Middle East democracy, it has been Facebook. With Christianity, it is the Holy Spirit.

Multiplication's primary strength is in making decisions that affect large populations and areas of society. Its weakness is that it is non-discriminatory. Evil is multiplied just as effectively as good.

Multiplication has been used in a rudimentary way in our world today. However, in secular societal development, its true power has not been tapped into because we only multiply with the vocabulary we know, which is still at the infant level of addition. Let me explain.

Here's an illustration of two people in a think tank, multiplying their thoughts. Each person's thoughts are enclosed in a bracket. If each person knew only the same four words and all their words were based on addition, the two people could collaborate and multiply for eight solutions.

$$(2 + 2) \times 2 = 8$$

If they had only words based on multiplication, they would multiply for the same eight solutions.

$$(2 \times 2) \times 2 = 8$$

So, what's the big deal? Same result, right? Well, let's up the ante a bit. What if each person had a two-hundred word vocabulary, instead of just four?

$$(100 + 100) \times 2 = 400, \text{ an additive vocabulary}$$

$$(100 \times 100) \times 2 = 20,000$$

The difference becomes even more striking, the greater the number of people in the think tank.

$(100 + 100) \times 120 = 24{,}000$ solutions

$(100 \times 100) \times 120 = 1{,}200{,}000$ solutions

Twenty four thousand solutions versus more than one million; pretty impressive difference, right?

Do we know any multiplicative words at all? And, if so, how frequently do we use them? Well, the answer to that depends on where you get your vocabulary from, and how much you use it.

When the Holy Spirit inhabited a hundred and twenty very ordinary people in Jerusalem on a feast day called Pentecost, all the multiplicative words ever made were now available to those one hundred and twenty men and women.

How did Christianity explode into an international religion that has changed empires, from a day two thousand years ago when a hundred and twenty ordinary people sat together in a room? The answer is really quite simple.

And these are they which are sown on good ground; such as hear the word, and receive it, and bring forth fruit, some thirtyfold, some sixty, and some an hundred. Mark 4:20.

DIVISION

Division, the hardest of the basic arithmetical skills, is all about supersets and subsets.

$21 / 3 = 7$

Therefore seven, called the quotient, is a subset of the superset, twenty-one.

Traditionally, division is grouped with multiplication, as it is indeed reverse multiplication. However, spiritually speaking, division is actually more closely related to sub-traction, which also identifies subsets.

$$21 - 14 = 7$$

Therefore seven, called the difference, is a subset of the superset, twenty-one.

The strength of spiritual division is that it recognizes patterns. There are shared characteristics between subsets and their parent supersets.

$$99 / 11 = 9, \text{ but } 9 / 3 = 3$$

Therefore, the subset of 3 has two supersets: the "little" superset of 9 and the bigger superset of 99. 3, 9, and 99 all share an intrinsic characteristic: None of them can be perfectly divided by 2.

These patterns enable one to make extrapolations about what will happen in little supersets—i.e., cities—and even bigger supersets—i.e., countries—when their people behave with certain characteristics. For example, the national debt is a superset of personal debt, and reflects the same behavior.

Spiritual division is primarily about pattern recognition, and closely is related to the spiritual gift of discernment and wisdom, or the, "Oh! I've seen that pattern before" phenomenon. It helps you understand problems so they can be solved, but also is very powerful in preventing them.

Jesus beautifully demonstrated spiritual division during one of his many discussions with the Pharisees.

Every kingdom divided against itself is brought to desolation; and every city or house divided against itself shall not stand. Matthew 12:25.

Here, kingdom is the "large" superset; city is the "little" superset; and house is the subset.

Another simple application of spiritual division is child behavior at school. The family is a small superset of the child. The school is a bigger superset of youth, in the families of that community. Beyond that, there are the even bigger supersets of county schools, and then the state's educational status.

Therefore, the key to solving violence and bullying in our schools is to stop siblings playing with firearms and punching each other in the head at home.

Now, our last example of this book comes from a famous Bible character. His name was King David of the "David and Goliath" story.

God chose David as a mere boy to be king when, as the last of his father's sons, he was left to take care of his father's sheep in the fields.

Why did God choose this young kid who, at the time of God's choice, did not look very kingly? Because God identified something in the boy, a hunger to think like God does. God saw a boy who chose to be his subset.

He raised up unto them David to be their king; to whom also he gave their testimony, and said, I have found David the son of Jesse, a man after mine own heart. Acts 13:22.

God's heart is love. People loved King David and he loved people; it's all over his story! God saw this in him and said, "This kid gets it; he gets *me!*" God is love and King of all kings. Therefore David, as God's subset, had no choice: David was a king.

God created man in his own image. Genesis 1:27.

The true believer is a subset of Almighty God, the superset.

How do I use this knowledge to my advantage today? Well, when I see a person who genuinely loves people and is well beloved of others, even if that person is poor, I now know who I'm looking at: I am looking at a queen, or a king.

When I find people whose legacy, long after they've gone, is filled with reminders of the good things they did while they were here, and continue to do for others today, I know I have found God's noble subsets. I do not need to meet them personally to make that determination. I have met their fruits. That's all I need to know.

If he called them gods, unto whom the word of God came, and the scripture cannot be broken. John 10:35.

We may not see it now, because we are using the wrong yardsticks of material blessings and birthright to measure a noble spirit. But once in eternity, it all will become quite clear. What will that look like? I honestly don't know. It is beyond my best imaginations of life and the fullest expression of it, forevermore. I'll just have to wait and see on graduation day.

EPILOGUE

J ust like that, it was done. He looked at the finished manuscript. The beginning almost felt like another lifetime, when a cheerful old man had wandered into his world, talking about thirds, the devil and Adolf Hitler.

Was that a true encounter, or did he just imagine it? The elastic band of one's imagination can birth both epiphanies and hallucinations; he knew that. But at this point, did it really matter? He had started, and he had finished. And God is love. There is nothing greater in heaven or earth; nothing more profound than that.

If he could leave a legacy to his children, it would be that singular truth. In fact, he already had started introducing the concept to them. He remembered talking with his little big boy a few nights ago. Smiling, he started writing again. He'd written so many stories; I guess there was space enough for one more.

The other day I asked my young son the following question: "What makes a person a king?"

Long pause. "I guess, a crown, and a throne?"

"So, if your dad bought a throne and a crown, would that make me a king?"

No pause this time. "No."

"I would think not."

"I guess a king has a lot of things, and people do what he says, I think."

So, changing tack, I painted a picture for him.

"What if you had no money and just a modest little home, but you could travel the world at will? You could go to all the places you ever dreamed about seeing, even live there for short periods of time, if you wanted.

"What if you never, ever had to worry about where to stay while you visit, because wherever you go, you could just walk into and be gladly welcomed in whatever house you chose? Welcomed with warm meals, a cozy bed, and people genuinely delighted to see you. Would you need money?"

A little bit of head scratching. "Enough to get me from place to place, I would."

"That's also free."

"Then, no. I wouldn't need money."

"Would you be living like a king?"

"Oh, yes."

"But you have no money!"

"I guess money doesn't make me a king."

"You guessed right. So, what does?" Leaning forward I earnestly engaged his gaze. "What would make people treat you like that? Would you treat your brother or your friend John like that?"

Without any hesitation, "Yes, I would."

"Why?"

"Because I love them!"

I slapped my knee enthusiastically.

"That's right! But why do you love them?"

"I'm not sure why. I just do."

"That's because you are older than both of them. What about your mother and I? Why do you love us?"

"Because you love and care about me." And then, cheekily: "Also because I have to."

"Careful, now!" Then getting serious again, "So, what makes a person a king?"

Illumination dawns in bright young eyes. "I get it now! By how he loves people and how they love him!"

"Yes, son, you get it now."

A king is made by how much he loves, not by how much he has.

The young nobleman-in-training had just learned his first lesson in spiritual discernment. As he strolled off to some other pursuit—I think it was dinner—I said quietly, in the hidden place where the mind speaks before ears hear the sound:

"Goodbye, young nobleman."

The kingdom of God is within you. Luke 17:21.

The truth always tells its own story, in time.

ACKNOWLEDGEMENTS

It took several years to finish this work, a new experience for me, but this only has served to make me more appreciative of the honor bestowed by our heavenly Father to spread his Word, through writing. Thank you, Father, for the privilege; I hope I have done you proud.

Thank you, Jesus Christ, my Lord and my King. You continue to reveal to me dimensions of yourself that make my heart break and yet, make my spirit sing. You are the reason that I'm alive to write these words.

Thank you, Holy Spirit, my comforter, teacher and friend. Without your counsel this work becomes a meaningless collection of words. You have made this book what it is. How could I have done it without you?

Thank you, Debrah, my wonderful wife and true companion. This labor of toil, sweat, and love has been supported by you in more ways than I can describe. You have been my first editor, a job that you have diligently carried out with patience and grace. I love you.

Thank you, Samuel and Daniel. Your lives and growth never cease to amaze me. God continues to show me slivers of himself through you. I'm proud to call you both my sons.

Thank you, Fiona Soltes, for your masterful editorial work, and Lightning Source Inc., without whom this work would not have been packaged and distributed in such an efficient manner. You will always have my gratitude.

Thank you, Mike, Sue, and "Mum," my parents and the rest of our family. You are a never-ending source of joy and wisdom to me. I think Mike's poem said in one page what it took me twenty pages to say! I have had the privilege of having you for all these years as a special gift from God. I pray fervently every night that God grants us many, many more.

Oh, and lastly, a special thanks to my brother Edwin, for perspectives on "rambling" and "verbosity." Cool insights! They were much appreciated!

THE BEAST, 2006

🕸

I t was a strange theory at best, but its very strangeness
kept him mulling it over. He shifted restlessly on the
couch, chewed the end of his pen and pondered the point.
Should he add it, or not?

If for nothing else, it made for some interesting debate.
Mountains could be continents cast into the sea. Therefore,
mountains could be continents, arising from the sea. The
elastic band of one's imagination. Anyway, the think tank
seemed to enjoy the idea. He recalled the earlier discussion.

"Hey guys, gather around. I had a thought."

Big Heart: "Another one? Here we go. What now?"

Quiet—maybe slightly deaf?—One: "Speak up; no
mumbling now. What you got?"

"All right, all right, I'll CRANK UP THE VOLUME!"
Laughter. "Anyway, seriously, you know the story of the
beast? The beast of the apocalypse, that fascinating point of
speculation? Well, there's that whole part about the Whore
of Babylon, decked in purple and scarlet, sitting upon a red
beast, with seven heads and ten horns. With the explanation
of the heads as mountains.

"There have been those theories that say that the Whore
of Babylon is the Catholic Church in Rome, and those heads
are the seven hills of Rome, over the Tiber River. I mean,
you can see the obvious reasons for this thinking: scarlet and

purple are the official adorning colors of the bishops, cardinals and pope; the jewels could allegorically indicate riches, the ornamental crosses and rings worn by the Catholic priests, the golden cup; etc.

Fiery One: "Yeah, I heard those theories. A lot of the thinking is that the Catholic Church is the whore."

Big Heart: "That's right."

"But then again, the Catholics have had a reasonable rebuttal: that the Vatican sits on 'Vatican Hill,' which is a hill on the opposite side of the Tiber River to the seven hills, that the word translated from the Greek to "mountains" does not correspond to translation of the Greek word for "hills." And that the Vatican is not rich."

"*Yeah, right!*"

Big Heart: "Mmm, hmm. And?"

"Well what if the mountains are the seven continents? What's described as a mountain is relative, right? A large body of land elevated far above your vantage point is a mountain. Or it could be a continent from sea level."

Quiet One: "Go on."

"Well, here goes: It is possible that the description of the beast as being the "eighth" might be an eighth *head* rather than an eighth king; an eighth mountain that comes from the other seven. I think the beast is the lost land of Atlantis."

Quiet One: "I knew you were going to say that! Once you started talking about continents."

"Think about it. The beast is described as the beast that was, is not, and yet is. If myth is true, Atlantis was, until it sank more than ten thousand years ago, no longer is, and yet still is buried deep under the sea."

Big Heart: "Haven't they found it already? I thought I heard something like that."

"They found some strange, energy-emitting rocks under the Atlantic; they have them at the University of Chicago or Washington, or somewhere. Some millionaire has spent a small fortune plotting out an area on the ocean floor that he believes is part of Atlantis.

"According to Plato's mythical story, they had a much more advanced civilization than we have, even today, with an alternative energy source. And that this was brought to earth by mythical extraterrestrials from another planet.

"Personally, I've always said that E.T.s, if they exist, are probably fallen angels, who appeared to man in a different form. Deception takes many shapes, and angels are shape-shifters after all, aren't they?"

Joywalker: "Yep. It just depends on how you interpret what you see."

"So, Atlantis is discovered and along with it, a technology and history that appears to predate the biblical creation of man. You see all those weird-looking archeologists from the Discovery and History channels? Suddenly, they are elevated to oracle status. Who is going to be the target, the most visible, organized Christian religious body that has unprecedented influence and followers all over the world? The Catholics."

The Fiery One: "Atlantis has to reappear for all that to happen, though."

"It will come up the same way it went down. With climate change from global warming, a huge earthquake is certainly within the realm of possibility. How about that large fault that runs through Indiana, down through Memphis, the New...?"

Big Heart: "The New Madrid Fault."

"That's the one. It has a greater than ninety percent chance of spawning an earthquake within the next twenty years. I was discussing it just the other day with a guy who has connections with State Farm Insurance. They are quite worried about the earthquake possibility. Estimates of the magnitude of that quake, if it occurs, will make Katrina, bad as it was, seem like a scraped knee."

"Insurance companies. Trying to wriggle out of payments as usual. They like to collect the premiums, though."

"You got that right."

"In all fairness, though, such a quake could bankrupt State Farm. Anyway, such a massive quake could cause massive tectonic plate shifts that could sink some land masses, raise others."

Joywalker: "How about the star falling to earth in Revelation?"

Big Heart: "A large meteor or asteroid falling to earth. That ought to shift things around a bit. A mere earth tremor rerouted the Mississippi a few years ago."

The Fiery One: "You just might be right."

"It's still just a thought, now. But it is quite plausible. After all, the second beast that comes from the land gives 'life' or 'spirit' to the first beast who arises from the sea. That implies that the first beast is lifeless to begin with. Because Beast Number One may be an inanimate object."

Quiet One: "You writing another book?"

Surprise. "Actually, yes."

Quiet One, with a knowing smile: "I thought so."

Big Heart: "You never know. This might be an important revelation for our times. Stranger things have been true."

So, here he was, back where he started. In or not? An important revelation for our times. Who knew? He pondered the implications.

The Catholic Church as the whore of Babylon?

He cringed at the idea of putting that in a book. Those were fighting words. He had close Catholic friends. He'd gone to a Catholic high school, stopped in midstride at midday, during Angelus, pretended to listen to the preaching of "Father Dowd," his school reverend. Even his mother had gone to school in a Catholic convent, even if she had not taken the sisterly vows.

But he knew about the times the same church had compromised and sold out, when they should have taken a stand: the Crusades, the Inquisition, the turning of a blind eye to the Holocaust. Most recently, the attempts to blur the requirements for priesthood, and the concealment and airbrushing of sexual abuse of young boys that is rotting the Catholic church from the inside out.

It is all to survive and continue to maintain self-image at all costs, even if it comes at the cost of integrity. Even if God has charged mankind to not to be overcome by evil, but to overcome evil with good. They would rather hope that two wrongs make a right, the true essence of a harlot, rather than the traditional raising of skirts.

Then, there was the name of blasphemy written on the whore's forehead. He couldn't help but remember Jesus Christ's warning:

And call no man your father upon the earth: for one is your Father, which is in heaven. Neither be ye called masters: for one is your Master, even Christ. Matthew 23:9.

Do not take God's name for yourself.

Why, then, would the Catholic Church choose to have its priests called "father" and the pope, the "Holy Father?" St. Peter the Apostle is accepted in Catholicism as the first pope. Yet, the apostle Peter, who walked the earth—and, briefly, the water—with Jesus Christ himself, and whom the pope and bishops are supposed to be direct successors of, in all the books of the Bible, was never called "Father Peter." Why on earth couldn't they just use another name, if "brethren" was not modern enough for them? Like "Buddy?"

Also there was the issue of the crosses and rings worn by the bishops. *Resplendent with jewels, of precious stones.* So, the Catholic Church is kind of asking for it.

But was the Protestant church to which I now belonged, be it Methodist, Anglican, Baptist, Pentecostal or, more recently, the hip "interdenominational," really any better? The turning of a blind eye to political deception, choosing partisanship rather than truth, supposedly to show God to the world? He remembered vividly the 2004 election year, the stem cell transplant controversy, the party and population split between pro-life and pro-choice.

He remembered the bright Saturday morning that he, as a potential concerned voter, decided to do some research of his own, on embryonic stem cell sources and adult stem cell transplantation.

It took a mere half day of research to find that pluripotent embryonic cells did not have to be harvested at the earliest stages of human development, a time that would destroy the whole embryo, that those cells could be taken much later from the placenta, when a fetus is several weeks old.

How many spontaneous miscarriages occur each year in the United States? Hundreds of thousands, the vast majority before twelve weeks of age, no more preventable than any accidental death.

It took a single curious man a mere half day to figure out that a request by hospital staff to harvest stem cells for research from this source, would probably have a higher yield, and less controversy than for traditional organ donation, after death. Democrats and Republicans could both have what they wanted. Why didn't anyone, even embryology experts, weigh in on the subject? Because deceit, on both sides, was the true agenda. But he didn't have a huge biff with that. After all, that is what politicians do.

The Republican candidate proudly, with no remorse whatsoever, announced that he had already released several cell lines of embryonic stem cells for research as the incumbent President. He just wasn't going to release any more lines. This was repeated several times, even in an address, in 2006. Not an apology before God or man; nothing. But he was one man, good or bad; Christian or not. He could make mistakes and be blinded by ambition and political pressure. It could happen to anyone; Jesus Christ made that clear, in Matthew 24.

Mercifully the tribulation period would be short, otherwise no-one would be saved, even the elect.

His problem was with the professed living church, to whom, according to the Gospels, much was given and, therefore, from whom much was expected. Jesus didn't waste words on the sins of Rome, either. It was the Jews he had harsh words for.

A kaleidoscope of interviews on Fox, CNN, MSNBC, with bishops, pastors, preachers, and evangelists flanked in interviews by newsmen, talk show hosts, and suddenly holy senators. The collective "Church" representation in the media, in churches, never once thought to gently state the truth. Correct a righteous man who had made a mistake or, alternatively, if it inconceivably was no mistake, expose the intentions of an evil pretender.

Integrity directed at a political figure cost John the Baptist his head; a lack of it will save the church's hide. But the words that come to mind are: *Whoesover shall love his life shall lose it and he who hates his life for Christ's sake will gain it.*

What use is your hide, if you've sold your soul? Then again, they would rather hope that two wrongs make a right, the true essence of a harlot.

The Catholic Church could be the Babylonian harlot. The first beast may be Atlantis, or something on it. And the second beast? He hadn't a clue.

May you live in interesting times.

What had he written earlier? Facts were not always truth. And the truth always tells its own story, in time. He decided: Better to be safe than sorry. It was just a theory, after all.

Besides, why cross the bridge when you can sit on it, and enjoy the view? If it was the truth, it could wait for another day.

CPSIA information can be obtained at www.ICGtesting.com
Printed in the USA
241654LV00003B/2/P